ENGLISH NATIONALSM

JEREMY BLACK

English Nationalism

A Short History

HURST & COMPANY, LONDON

First published in the United Kingdom in 2018 by
C. Hurst & Co. (Publishers) Ltd.,
41 Great Russell Street, London, WC1B 3PL
© Jeremy Black, 2018
All rights reserved.
Printed in India

Distributed in the United States, Canada and Latin America by
Oxford University Press, 198 Madison Avenue, New York,
NY 10016, United States of America.

The right of Jeremy Black to be identified as the author of
this publication is asserted by him in accordance with the
Copyright, Designs and Patents Act, 1988.

A Cataloguing-in-Publication data record for this book
is available from the British Library.

ISBN: 9781849049856

This book is printed using paper from registered sustainable
and managed sources.

www.hurstpublishers.com

For
Roger Kimball

CONTENTS

PREFACE

Readers wishing to engage with the meat of the book should 'Immediately Advance to Go' and turn at once to the Introduction. This Preface provides a personal note that may not be of importance and interest to others. With their emphasis on source-based work, historians are trained to be objective, and to sink their own personality from sight. Personal engagement is disapproved of, and understandably so if you are writing about an eighteenth century you can never visit or readily experience. At the same time, detachment can be pushed beyond the bounds of what the reader wants. I have long received comments, if not complaints, about writing in an impersonal voice—'It can be argued'—and being too keen on the approach of 'On the one hand... on the other'. Indeed, I have, in turn, criticised the alternative 'argument by assertion' approach that appears to characterise all too many writers, both historians and political commentators.

These methodological and stylistic points prove of particular relevance in this topic as it is one in which not only are many readers strongly engaged emotionally, but also they appear to expect a clear commitment by the writer in what they read. This situation has been taken further in the furore that accompanied and followed the United Kingdom's Brexit referendum of 2016. In many respects, this issue became a classic instance of the past being approached, debated, and understood, in terms of the present, and to an extent that drove out other perspectives. The present both set the terms of what was of interest, and greatly affected the responses of readers, thus providing a clear example of the politicisation of history.

Some will argue that there is an inherent politicisation in history, and, linked to this, that everything that historians write is subjective. This commonplace view, however, while understandable in terms of the stress on what to study and how to approach it, can only be taken so far, because there are events that happened, even if varied degrees of knowledge about what happened: you can say to me that China bombed Pearl Harbor in 1940, and I can tell you that Japan did it in 1941. Moreover, these events occurred for reasons, and explanations of them are not of equal accuracy. Everyone is entitled to an opinion, but not all opinions are equal.

An incremental, one hopes balanced, approach to trying to offer an objective account of the past, however, appears unwelcome to individuals who grasp and deploy it in the cause of present commitment. Furthermore, they do so from across the political spectrum. I have certainly found this to be the case with this book. I was aware that the subject was contentious, but have been struck by the single-mindedness and stridency with which, in conversation or correspondence, many have treated it. This has also been accompanied by a marked shrinking and foreshortening of the historical, cultural, and social frame of reference.

To many, the issue was defined not only by themselves and their experiences, but also by the events of very recent years. In this approach, English nationalism was a creation only of those years, and was defined in a partisan fashion accordingly. The earlier world of the Anglo-Saxon, 'Old English', monarchy of the tenth and eleventh centuries, or the Tudor England of the Protestant Reformation and the plays of William Shakespeare, were not mentioned. Others, indeed, had an awareness of a 'deep history' or long-term structural existence to English nationalism, but they were a tiny minority. In some cases, but far from invari ably, this difference was related to political opinions on Brexit. It is rarely automatic that a reading can be made from current poli tics to historical views, and vice versa. At the same time, there is frequently a correlation.

To this historian, the question might fairly be phrased, or rephrased, in terms of the relevance of the 'deep history' to recent, current, and future contentions. This can be taken further by ask ing whether 'deep history' was, is, and will be, reshaped by current concerns. So, yes, allowing for a 'deep history,' there is a long standing English nationalism, but what does it mean, and, sepa rately, does it matter? The use of the battle of Bannockburn (1314) by Scottish nationalists showed that a 'deep history' can be made relevant, with the Scottish discussion of the historical merits of independence perforce focusing on the centuries when Scotland was a separate state; but there has been no comparable English reference to the historical defiance of foreign invaders, whether Norman in 1066, French in 1216, or Spanish in 1588. Instead, the frame of historical reference is far shorter, namely that of the last century, and thus focused on the British experience. The key inva sion of note is that threatened by Germany in 1940.

These are among the topics I address in this book. I have already written histories of the British Isles, Britain, England, and Wales, either from start to finish, or for part of their chro nology. I cannot expect that they have all, or any, been read by readers of this work, so there is a degree of repetition in it. Nevertheless, this is a new book, and I have not addressed this question at length before.

The approach is essentially chronological, although the intro ductory chapter attempts to introduce some main themes from start to finish. A key one is that national consciousness is a

PREFACE

'hegemonic' concept, in that states, and 'peoples' or nations, are rarely united with shared views and a common purpose; although national myths about present identity and past history generally pretend otherwise and will doubtless continue to do so. So also with the concept of the *zeitgeist* (spirit of the age), and the related one, for those who differ from the alleged *zeitgeist*, of false consciousness.

Turning to the past, as public politics—especially those associated with a representative system (Parliament in the English case), and, later, with a culture of print—led to a discourse of national consciousness, the need to define such a concept in an acceptable fashion increased. It was more clearly politicised, taken from the literary discourse of nationhood that had been characteristic of the later medieval period, and given a number of competing partisan interpretations. This was readily apparent from the sixteenth century, although it would be mistaken to underrate the extent and politicisation of national identity in the fifteenth. It is, however, important to try to move from the partisanship linked to politicisation, past or present-day, when addressing this topic in a scholarly fashion.

I have found this an invigorating book. Some may believe it demonstrates that historians are out of touch. I would prefer to suggest that, aside from its inherent interest, the relevance of the past and of its consideration emerge far more strongly from this book. So does the difficulty of defining national identity and interests.

* * *

I have benefited greatly from the willingness of others to comment on earlier drafts and to discuss the topic with me. The former, who have given much time to the task, include John Blair, Eileen Cox, Patrick Deane, Bill Gibson, David Gladstone, James Kellock, Augusta Kyte, Stephen Perring, Nigel Saul,

PREFACE

Robert Smith, Peter Spear, Richard Toye, Peter Ward, Stuart Ward, and two anonymous readers. The latter group includes Stephen Badsey, Graham Brady, Melvyn Bragg, Ian Cook, James Davey, Glenn Hall, Jaye Guest, Harry Hyman, Max King, Nick Lewis, Nadine Majaro, Marc-William Palen, Azzie and Derek Partridge, Fred Roberts, William Salomon, Stephanie Speakman, Ulf Sundberg, Robin Swinburne, David Ward, and Jonathan West. It has been a great pleasure to work with Michael Dwyer and his colleagues at Hurst on this book.

I benefited from being appointed to the body that reviewed the National Curriculum for history teaching in English and Welsh schools. I also enjoyed the opportunity to speak on this and related topics at the University of Exeter, and, more particularly, at a conference held in New York and organised by the *New Criterion*. I take great pleasure in dedicating this book to its editor, Roger Kimball, a fine scholar, perceptive critic, erudite and fluent commentator, and someone whose friendship I have enjoyed now for nearly two decades.

INTRODUCTION

What is happening to the United Kingdom, and, within that, what is happening to England? This book looks to the past in order to try to understand the present; namely, what forces have shaped the historical identity of England and how that has affected English nationalism today.

Nationalism is a feeling as much as a principle. It manifests powerful emotional elements as well as the interaction of the 'deep histories' of particular national, or would-be national, groups with the contexts and expressions of these 'deep histories' in specific circumstances. These 'deep histories' are the understanding of the past that is central to identity as well as being an expression of this idea. The contexts include geography, climate, culture, society, economics and politics, and the experiences and expressions of each of these.

Englishness is an identity, a consciousness, and, at present, a proto-nationalism. It is the latter because there is currently no English state within the United Kingdom, which is the United Kingdom of Great Britain and Northern Ireland. Great Britain (Britain for short) itself is composed of England, Scotland, and

Wales. England is the largest and, by far, the most populous part of Britain and of the United Kingdom, but it is only part of the whole. There is no English passport, Parliament or currency, nor any immediate prospect of any. Moreover, there is relatively little that is distinctive to England within Great Britain or the United Kingdom, and notably so since the relative decline in significance of the Church of England. Despite the American tendency to refer to the 'Queen of England,' the monarch rules the United Kingdom.

That, however, does not mean that England lacks an identity, or identities. Moreover, nationalism, or at least a distinctive nationalism, has been precipitated, and, in part, forced upon England, by the development in the British Isles of strident nationalisms that have contested Britishness, and with much success. Irish nationalism was the first, but it was followed by those of Wales and, more prominently, Scotland.

This crystallisation of identity raises the question of how far back in time one can project a form of English nationalism. If statehood is the key issue, then the creation of the Old English (Saxon) monarchy in the tenth century is critical, as that produced an English state. Moreover, from 1066 (as well as under the Romans and King Cnut), as part of a larger political realm, the English state continued until it ended with the merger of the English and Scottish parliaments in 1707.

So that is one history of English nationalism, a history made complex by the need to discuss, prior and subsequent to 1707, the consequences of being part of a larger realm. The second approach is to look at a more recent foundation, as suggested above, one that reflects a decline in Britishness. There is no unanimously correct answer. Each approach is relevant and has its merits.

Part of the problem, but also the answer, is suggested by the nature and extent of multiple identities, by the beliefs and wishes they encompass, and by the degree to which these factors vary across time. These multiple identities can be readily seen today, and were also manifested in the past. The *Evening Standard* of 10 October 2017 published the results of a study by Queen Mary College, University of London, based on a YouGov poll of 1,044 Londoners, which revealed that 46 per cent of those surveyed named 'Londoner' as their primary identity; 25 per cent European; 17 per cent British; and only 12 per cent English. These results were qualified by the question of how strongly they felt each of these identities on a scale of zero to ten—one not available hitherto for historic discussion of multiple identities. Londoner came top (7.7), followed by British (7.4), English (6.6), and European (4.9). People in London who voted in 2016 to leave the European Union felt slightly more British than they did Londoner, with scores of 7.9 and 7.7; European scored 2.5.

London, however, is both a vital part of England, and yet is also atypical in its mix of people and politics. So while Englishness as a political idea in the 2010s is in part a response to the rise of the Scottish Nationalist Party, it is also partly a revolt against a London-dominated account of Englishness. This was highlighted by the role of Brexit, as London, atypically within England other than university towns, backed the Remain cause and has remained a centre of Remain sentiment since.

Multiple identities exist more broadly than with regard to nationalism, geography and ethnicity. They also relate to one's position in the family, for example as both parent and child. Here, however, the focus is geography and nationalism, which constitute part of the aggregate identity of both England and Britain. In parallel to the argument that there exists a particularly strong identity, there is the reality of multiple and overlapping identities, with neither 'multiple' nor 'overlapping' providing much guidance to priorities in the event of tensions or clashes. Conflicting identities also exist: one can be both a a member of the 'Church of England' in Scotland or Wales, or a Scot who seeks independence from Britain.

The co-existence of multiple identities has been revealed in the polls, and should usefully be extrapolated onto the past. If the 2014 Scottish referendum, in which independence was rejected, and the 2017 Scottish results in the general election, which saw a decline in the SNP vote, suggested the ability to be Scottish and British, with a consequent history of Scottish identity, then it is unclear why the same should not be true for England: it should be possible to be both English and British. That raises the question whether the standard contemporary liberal critique of Englishness as 'extreme' (i.e. politically partisan), or un-British, is misjudged. At present, hostility to 'England,' whatever that is supposed to mean, is part of the intellectual baggage of the age, both in the British Isles and abroad. The latter is possibly because England is seen as the wellspring of the British Empire. Looked at differently, in the nineteenth and early twentieth centuries, the English (but not generally the Scots) said England when they meant Britain. The *Oxford History of England*, the major series on national history, was defined as a study of Britain. Possibly the attenuation, and even ending, of the relationship between England and Scotland will make it easier to say England when meaning England.

Separate issues include the degree to which nationalism and patriotism are interchangeable terms and, if not, what the distinction amounts to, and means, and for whom? There is the question of the extent to which Englishness means not only different values in particular parts of England, but also has varied consequences, not least in terms of the intensity with which it is held. A lack of awareness about other parts of England is often thrown at Londoners. In 1980, indeed, when I was appointed to a university post in Durham, my mother, a Londoner, assumed that it must be in southern England because she knew that it had a fine cathedral and the other cathedral cities of which she was aware (Canterbury, Chichester, Salisbury, Wells and Winchester) were all in the South: so much for York! Ridiculous perhaps, but the ignorance of the South (and hostility towards it) held by Northerners can also be extreme. Each has a tendency to agglomerate, simplify and misrepresent the other. At the same time, there are changes across time. For example, Scottish tension with England now focuses on London and the 'South-East,' rather than, as in the fourteenth and sixteenth centuries, when war was to the fore, on northern England.

The situation at present can be with reason, and certainly is with rhetoric, contested from a variety of political, indeed politicised, stances. Thus, pretty well everything interpretive in what follows invites debate. So also does the selection of what to cover. Inevitably, there will also be suggestions that the author has conscious or (more interesting) unconscious biases, and notably so as someone who is English and lives in England, indeed only working outside England for six months: in Scotland in 1975.

A more valid critique would be that author and readers are affected by the contexts of the present. That certainly captures the degree to which our questions, and possibly our answers, reflect the issues of concern at the moment. Indeed, the very decision to write on English nationalism is both a reflection of trends in recent decades, notably the rise of Scottish and Welsh nationalism, and, more particularly, events in recent years, particularly the Scottish independence referendum of 2014 and the Brexit referendum of 2016. Each was very much a product of contingency in terms of timing, causes and results. The Brexit referendum for many appears to have swallowed the 2014 referendum as an issue, and led to the argument that a Brexit that, because of the distribution of the vote in 2016, is really an Exit (departure due to English votes), will force England to rethink its identity.[1] However, in practice, it was the 2014 referendum that made

Englishness an issue of particular interest and urgency. Moreover, Scottish independence remains significant as an issue, indeed is becoming more so as a result of the Brexit referendum.

In 2014, the dissolution of the British state, albeit with an independent Scotland having the same monarch, appeared possible, even briefly probable, as a result of the referendum on Scottish independence. The very possibility of such an outcome reflected a markedly different present-day background to the past, to that which would have been the case only twenty years earlier. Indeed, the Scottish Parliament that helped to make this referendum an issue was only established following an earlier referendum held in 1997 after the Labour victory in the general election held earlier that year. The first elections for this new Parliament occurred in 1999. As predicted, Labour formed the government in Edinburgh, but the SNP formed a minority government in 2007 and then a majority one in 2011. Labour has continued to be outplayed by the SNP in Scotland, even when it did better than before in the 2016 general election.

What the 2014 referendum might mean for England became a matter of debate. Suggestions included that the English themselves should have a vote on the matter, with some proposing, and not always flippantly, that they would vote for Scottish independence. This argument was an instructive one as it presupposed not only a separate English identity, but also that it should have a degree of agency. In 2016, in the Brexit referendum, 62 per cent of the Scots who voted opted to remain in the EU, which underlined the grave tensions in UK politics and identity. As a result of this referendum, a view about being in the wrong country was increasingly expressed by Scots as an automatic response to what was seen as the wrong destiny.

Timing is important to the approach taken. The extent to which English nationalism has a 'deep history' is a matter of controversy, or at least of emphasis; although this book seeks to

INTRODUCTION

demonstrate that there is such a history. The significance of this
'deep history' for more recent centuries is also controversial. If a
long-term geopolitical, political, and constitutional viewpoint is
adopted, there was an independent English state by the mid-
tenth century. There was also such a state, that included Wales,
but was separate from an independent Scottish state, by 1320, by
when the independence of Scotland was clearly established and
the rulers of England had not yet embarked on their campaign
to rule France or regain Normandy. In England and in Scotland
in the thirteenth century, moreover, as an aspect of political
power and consciousness, there were limits to royal power and
authority. In England, as an important grounding of nationalism,
at least in the shape of national consciousness and exceptionalism, there was a well-developed representative system in the
shape of Parliament, while freedoms were grounded in the
Common Law.

Such an approach, with its emphasis on origins and early
developments, corresponds to the focus on early republican history in American history, specifically the Founding Fathers of
independence. This focus in American history, however, has
been recently challenged by a different narrative that concentrates
on later immigration, civil rights, and the history of the last
century-and-a-half, and indeed the period from the New Deal in
the 1930s. The question of a similar, foreshortened, or end-
loaded, coverage for English (and indeed British) history is readily apparent and can also raise questions about bias on the part
of the historian.

More seriously, there are the difficulties of distinguishing
English history from its British counterpart. If the key structural
elements in the case of England, most obviously, are island status
off the shore of a nearby continent, as well as the proximity of
most of the country to the sea and to ports, then this is as much
the case for Scotland, Wales and, even more, Ireland (or indeed

7

Japan), as for England. So also with the distinctiveness of society and political culture. The characteristic nature and role of law, property rights, family structure, and political liberty, have all been regarded as crucial to English society and political culture, but all, bar the legal system, were also true of Scotland. Scotland also shared in the Whiggish triumphalism, the sense that developments were inevitable and praiseworthy, that was very much seen in England in the eighteenth and nineteenth centuries.

British identity and nationalism overlapped with those of England, but with a very different chronology. 'Rule Britannia, Rule the waves, Britons never will be slaves,' James Thomson's linkage of national destiny, naval strength and personal liberty for the masque *Alfred* (1740), remained resonant while Britain was the world's leading maritime power. They looked towards 1902 when Arthur Benson's words for 'Land of Hope and Glory', the third of Edward Elgar's *Pomp and Circumstance* marches, were first heard as part of the *Coronation Ode* for Edward VII (r. 1901–10), the great-grandfather of Elizabeth II (r. 1952–).

Thomson's lines, produced at a time of war with Spain, that of Jenkins' Ear (1739–48), exemplify the extent to which much of the expression of national identity was focused on antipathy to what was constructed as a different world, that of Continental autocracy and Catholicism. Antipathy, or at least definition in opposition to..., is a key element in nationalism as nationhood is given political force. National identity indeed was moulded during war with France and Spain. There was declared war with the former in 1689–97, 1702–13, 1744–8, 1756–63, 1778–83, 1793–1802, 1803–14 and 1815, undeclared war in 1743–4 and 1754–6, and hostile relations at other times, for example 1714–16, 1731–42, 1787 and 1790. There was war with Spain in 1718–20, 1739–48, 1761–3, 1779–83, 1796–1802, and 1803–8. This was the context, as the historian Linda Colley noted in her influential book *Britons: Forging the Nation, 1707–1837* in which British identity was created and Empire expanded.

INTRODUCTION

Just as English identity had owed much to conflict with the Danes from the late ninth century to the late eleventh and, subsequently, to the Hundred Years' War with France (1337–1453), to the sense of war with Catholicism stemming from the Protestant Reformation, and to war with Spain from 1585 to 1604 and again in the 1620s and 1650s; so the new creation of Britain was baptised in talk of values at war with those of France. The experience of the Napoleonic Wars in particular underscored a patriotic discourse on British distinctiveness whilst simultaneously creating a new iconography of national military heroes focused on Abercromby, Moore, Nelson, and Wellington, one that replaced Marlborough and Wolfe. In the 1800s, *God Save the King* came to be called the National Anthem.

The resonance of these wars was longstanding with London, national and imperial capital, the setting for a memorialisation of identity through victory. Nelson's Column, Waterloo Station, the tombs of national heroes in St Paul's Cathedral, the Trafalgar and Waterloo anniversary dinners, Wellington's funeral: these sites and occasions contributed directly to a staging and drama of national exceptionalism. It was one that left a ready legacy in street names across the country. So also with the calendar which has left a varied number and character of commemorative dates, including St George's Day (as well as St Patrick's, St David's and St Andrew's), Guy Fawke's Day, Oak Apple Day, the Last Night of the Proms, and the Royal British Legion Festival of Remembrance.

At the same time, the nineteenth century also saw a fleshing out of a sense of national greatness that did not focus so closely on triumph in war. Victorian Britain displayed attitudes of national uniqueness, nationalist self-confidence, and a xenophobic contempt for foreigners, especially Catholics, but also Arabs, Jews, Turks and Africans. This xenophobia was not generally a matter of hostility towards foreignness itself (although that factor was definitely involved), but rather to what was seen as backward and illiberal. The latter were defined in accordance with English/ British criteria, and thus English Catholics and Jews could share in these opinions, but these criteria were also seen as of wider applicability and for all people. Religious toleration, freedom of speech, and a free press, were all regarded as important. Alongside this xenophobia, there was a more general sense of superiority to other cultures, notably Catholic ones but also Protestant counterparts. Moreover, the expansion of British power meant that there was a need to respond to cultures about which little was hitherto known, for example those of China and Japan.

Parliamentary government was regarded as a key characteristic of a Britishness that was essentially English, one that Britain exported to its Dominions overseas. Thus, the Parliament building in Ottawa was similar to that in London, as was that in Budapest, which was never part of the Empire. This process was appropriate because Britain, and later the United Kingdom in 1801, was created by Act of Parliament, and thus by the politics that led to that Act and which were expressed in terms of a new British Parliament. The unitary state of Great Britain was established on 12 May 1707 as a result of the union of England and Scotland. This step was intended as a union far deeper than the union of the Crowns in 1603 when James VI of Scotland also became James I of England, and was seen as a more permanent union as it was believed that the latter could dissolve if the crowns of England and Scotland went different ways after the death of Queen Anne (r. 1702–14). After the death of the unmarried and childless William, Duke of Gloucester in 1701, she had no surviving children. As a reminder of the precariousness of personal unions, that of the crowns of Portugal and Spain had collapsed in 1640 as a result of rebellion in Portugal, although the subsequent war lasted until 1668.

Britain was in part a parliamentary creation, unlike the very different entities of England and Scotland; although Wales was

INTRODUCTION

in large part governmentally constructed when it was incorporated into the English realm under an Act of Parliament in 1536. Northern Ireland, itself, as a result of the Anglo-Irish treaty in 1921, linked to Britain in the United Kingdom, is a relic of the Act of Union with Ireland which came into force in 1801. Britain, the united expression of what would otherwise have been a federal state, lacks a deep history comparable to England, Scotland and, far less clearly as a political unit, Wales. Indeed, much that we associate with one is of no relevance for the others or an other. Magna Carta (1215), a key event in English history, means nothing in Scotland; while, conversely, the Declaration of Arbroath (1320) was a crucial foundation moment in Scottish, but not English, history.

Moreover, common processes, such as the Roman attack in the first century, the 'Barbarian' invasions of the fifth to eleventh centuries, feudalism in the eleventh to thirteenth centuries, the Protestant Reformation of the sixteenth century, and the civil wars of the 1640s, played out very differently in the distinct states of the British Isles and for their nations, as they also did across Western Europe. Indeed, the relevant units for the Reformation are as much France and Scotland, or England and Sweden, as Britain. Thus, despite retrospective and sometimes successful attempts to create a common memory, there was none, even if there was a powerful need to respond to similar circumstances, events and, eventually, from 1603, rulers.

This is a key point in the modern struggle over national identity, as many Scots and Welsh correctly see their identity, like that of England, as more historically grounded than that of Britain. As a result, to begin British history prior to 1707 is in part a legacy of the politics, government, and culture created by the Act of Union. It is therefore a political legacy of a certain period, an approach of dubious historical value, and one that may look increasingly invalid as separatism increases. Instead, the period prior to 1707 includes centuries crucial for English history and nationalism.

This point directs attention to whatever is meant by Englishness. If Britishness is a time-limited, essentially (or is it originally?) political, concept, and of value within a state shaped by very different historical legacies, and with individuals and communities holding multiple identities, then it becomes necessary to consider what to make of Englishness. This is the case whether or not Britain collapses, and the latter helps to move the debate away from the referendum on Scottish independence. Englishness thus becomes at once identity and analytical tool, at once a state of consciousness and a product of it, and yet also a potentially important rhetorical means in culture and debate.

Starting British history at 1707 puts the focus on a world that is not as remote as if searching for political or cultural origins in Anglo-Saxon (and Scottish and Welsh) forests, which was where seventeenth-century English commentators searched for the origins of English liberty. Indeed, there was much already in existence in the 1700s, and newly confirmed by the terms of the Union of 1707 and the politics of the surrounding decades. Much of this seems somehow familiar. The ideas of limited government, representative politics, accountable monarchy, the rule of law, and an absence of religious persecution (Catholics would not have agreed), were all well-established. Indeed, partly as a result, they have been all part of Britain's 'deep history,' with particularly long-lasting roots in at least part of Britain.

Thus, English Common Law, with its stress on trial by jury and on equality before and under the law, was an important aspect of English distinctiveness, looking back to the Anglo-Saxon period, and, from the twelfth century, this was true of both the content of the law and the way it was administered. Common Law was particularly suited to the protection of rights and liberties, and, as a process referential toward the past, and reverential of it, the Common Law encouraged a respect for the character and continuity of English political society. At the same time, the legal tradition was very different in Scotland where there was a basis, instead, in Roman law.

Legal and political practices were not simply those of constitutional and political force, but also reflected and sustained assumptions that constitute essential aspects of a history handed on to immigrants and to new generations, notably a belief in fairness, in freedoms, and in accountability. These assumptions provide an historical basis for a democratic culture in British history. This culture is therefore not simply grounded in constitutional provisions, such as Magna Carta, the Declaration of Arbroath, and the restrictions on royal authority that followed the expulsion of James II (of England) and VII (of Scotland) in 1688–9, in the so-called Glorious Revolution. This expulsion, and the possibility it opened up of England and Scotland moving apart, with different monarchs, was the key background to an Act of Union established by Parliament.

Partly as a result (although modern British democratic cultures, as well as their components, English, Scottish and Welsh, are not particularly acute in their knowledge of historical facts, as opposed to collective myths), these cultures reflect, nevertheless, a pervasive historicism of continuing values, values that are grounded in past events and practices. More specifically, the instance of William of Orange's successful invasion of England in 1688 leading to Union in 1707 raises interesting parallels to what may flow from the disruptions and uncertainties of 2014–18.

Although the quest for freedom (both political and religious), the growth of democracy, the defence of liberty, and the respect for law and individual rights, do not provide both narrative and analysis for the entire thrust of British (and English) history, they do manage this for important episodes of which the British (and English) are proud. These episodes are then joined, and notably so in England, to present an account of a benign progress towards liberty, in what is referred to as the Whig interpretation of British (and English) history, a view that is the basis to the way in which the British (and English) have tended to present their history. Adding here 'and English' adds in a throwaway phrase that is potentially unhelpful. The phrase underplays the extent to which Britain is in part an expression of Englishness, certainly to many of the English, but also as a result of the past historical success of the English state in the British Isles and of England within the British state.

Moreover, this quest, this defence, and this aspect, do offer a noteworthy example to the present and, more generally, across the world. It is the peculiar greatness of British (and English) history that those who fought gloriously for national independence, most especially in 1805 (the Trafalgar campaign) against Napoleon and in 1940 (the Battle of Britain) against Hitler, were also asserting values that were more noble and uplifting than those of the nation's enemies. So also for the English opposition to Philip II of Spain in 1588, the year of the Spanish Armada. Given that national identity was reliant on opposition to others, this situation was highly significant.

In contrast, there is an uneasiness about aspects of British imperial past, notably its leading role in the Atlantic slave trade in the eighteenth century, one that began with England in the sixteenth century. It is one of the ironies of British history that the country also played the leading role in ending that trade in the nineteenth century, legislating against first the slave trade and then slavery; and then using the Royal Navy and diplomatic pressure to try to stamp out both across the world.

This double role indicates the extent to which the national past can resonate with very different themes. That also serves as a reminder that what is stressed tends to reflect current interests and needs. Thus, the governmental emphasis in the 2000s and

INTRODUCTION

2010s on Britishness represented a deliberate attempt to strengthen
and sustain a sense of national identity in the face of what were
seen as challenging tendencies, notably large-scale immigration
and the rise of radical Islam. The problem posed by the latter
was driven home with terrorist attacks in London in 2005, and
further underlined by more, notably in 2017 in both London and
Manchester.

Yet, at the same time, as a reminder of the range of explanations possible for many historical episodes, the policy of sup-
porting devolution can be discussed not so much as due to the
SNP but rather in terms of the determination of the Labour
governments of 1997–2010, heavily reliant on Scottish support,
to resist the separation of England and Scotland advanced by the
Scottish Nationalists, as well as to oppose calls for greater commitment to English interests. Thus, the language of Britishness
under the Tony Blair (1997–2007) and, even more, the Gordon
Brown (2007–10) governments became an assertion of long-term
values very much in relation to the political needs and cultural
fashions of the present day, as with 'Cool Britannia'. With the
creation in 1997 of a Scottish Parliament and Executive, however,
the drift was apparently very much away from a British identity.
Just as it was created by Act of Parliament, so it may well be
dissolved by another, with, yet again, Parliaments in Edinburgh
and London playing the key role. Looked at differently, another
type of Britishness, a more federal type, was a prospect. The
latter suggested a new role for English consciousness, whether by
intention or by circumstance. Moreover, what Englishness might
mean in a post-Brexit United Kingdom was unclear.

Whatever the future, the long tradition of British history that
prevailed for a quarter-millennium from the Act of Union with
Scotland has largely collapsed in recent decades. Empire disappeared, particularly from the granting of independence to India
in 1947, as, soon after, did Britain's leading maritime rule.

Indeed, it became apparent that British history in many respects had meant British Empire history, and much of it ended with the loss of Empire. Until 1947, Britishness was quintessentially Imperial. As a result, the 'Little Britishness' characteristic of the post-war period is of very recent origin and not as deeply-rooted as is generally implied. Part of the debate about Britishness today is reminiscent of earlier discussions about what Britain might mean if Empire collapsed.

From a different political perspective, and again addressing change, all too much of the quest for freedom, defence of liberty, and respect for law and individual rights, that the English and British saw as their legacy have been neglected or distorted in recent decades by governmental and institutional priorities and interests. In particular, a combination of the communitarian solutions pushed politically, the inroads of European federalism, and a lack of trust in the individual, has transformed the political and legal culture of the country. Parliamentary government was eroded, or at the very least altered, by the rise of European institutions, notably the European Parliament and courts, and by the incorporation of European law. Accountability changed.

Indeed, in 1993, a leading English historian, W.A. Speck, published a *Concise History of Britain, 1707–1975* in which he claimed that his chronology 'spans the whole history of Britain in the precise sense' as membership of what became the European Union was, he argued, a partial surrender of British sovereignty. This sense of discontinuity carried forward the 1962 remark by Hugh Gaitskell, the leader of the Labour Party, then in opposition, that such membership would mean 'the end of Britain as an independent nation'. Speck, a proud Yorkshireman, was on the Left. Thus, for Gaitskell, Speck, and others, the recent past had/has very much seen a recasting of the legacy of the distant past with the two being linked. Whereas some changes, notably the end of Empire, have not led to much of a sense of dislocation for many Britons, particularly those who did not experience imperial greatness, this was not the case as far as European integration is concerned.

A failure to appreciate the degree of reframing in recent history represents a key misunderstanding of Britain's and England's past. Alongside many Britons, foreigners (whether or not tourists), sold by the 'heritage industry' an impression of ancient ceremonial, historic cities, and long continuity, have often failed to appreciate not only that most British or English people neither have tea with the Queen nor commit murders in picturesque villages, the latter always set in southern England, but also that in recent decades there have been sweeping changes, notably in culture, society, and living arrangements.

But that is not the sole misunderstanding. There is also a tendency to see British and English history as interchangeable; indeed of Britain as a greater or another England. Both of these approaches are in part true, but are also far from automatically the case. This misunderstanding is shared by many of the English, although it is one that is far more valid from their perspective than from that of many Scots. As already noted, the idea that Magna Carta, with its criticisms of the autocratic governance of King John and its affirmation of different standards, is a key date carries scant weight with the Scots. Magna Carta resonated with English parliamentary critics of the autocratic government of Charles I (r. 1625–49), but his Scottish opponents looked to a very different tradition in Church and State.

There is, of course, no perfect balance in the history of Britain. For example, the 'four nations' approach to the history of the British Isles (English, Scots, Welsh, Irish), which has been highly fashionable, as well as politically expedient, since the 1980s, devotes insufficient attention to England, which is by far the preponderant nation in terms of population, wealth and power. Linked to this point, there is also a more general failure in histories of Britain, or indeed England, to devote sufficient space to the history of the localities and regions of England.

There is also an overly-critical and somewhat ahistorical account of Empire, one that reflects the extent to which the overthrowing of British rule is important to the foundation accounts of so many states, for instance India. In particular, there is a failure to understand the extent to which Britain, or, as far as imperialism within the British Isles was concerned, England, were not the sole imperial power, nor the conqueror of native peoples ruling themselves in a democratic fashion. There is also a misleading tendency to blame British imperial rule for many of the pressures and problems stemming from modernisation and globalisation. As an Empire, Britain engaged with rival empires, notably Nazi Germany, that are correctly seen as tyrannies. Empire gave Britain the strength to win.

Another source of criticism of Britain, and more particularly England, stems from its association with outdated social and political practices, notably social division, class control, and the role of the monarchy. The balanced constitution on which eighteenth and nineteenth-century British commentators prided themselves, a constitution praised by many contemporary foreigners, is now rejected by many commentators as an undesirable legacy for a democratic age.

This approach has been taken further in the world of Hollywood in which the British, even more English, repeatedly appear as the villainous opponents of democratic tendencies, as well as being personally, psychologically, and sexually, repressed and repressive. A cut-glass English accent is frequently the sign of a villain, a longstanding tendency seen from the 1930s, and one given new possibilities today in the age of prominent Old Etonian actors.

Again, this account of the past is flawed, mainly because it simplifies the past, giving it a misleading aggregate description, while also inscribing against the British, more specifically

English, characteristics that might be more generally unattractive in the modern democratic age, but not so prior to then. Yet, the strength of visual impressions in films such as *Braveheart* (1995), *The Patriot* (2000), or *Pirates of the Caribbean* (five films 2003–17), works far more powerfully on modern audiences than the balancing arguments of scholars.

So also, more insidiously, does the impression, created by television, film, and historical novels, that people in the past were like us. This is an approach particularly seen with the rendition of classic novels, such as those of Jane Austen, Charles Dickens, Anthony Trollope (all English) among others. It is also seen with reconstruction dramas based on life in the past. This approach removes the distance of the past and encourages the view that people should have behaved like us. Thus, when they did or do not, they can be criticised, or made to appear quaint or ridiculous. Britain, of course, is not alone in receiving this treatment. However, the approach is particularly pronounced in the treatment of British history because of the strength and accessibility of Britain's literary tradition and the extent to which this tradition has become common property, in large part because of the relationship between the United States, notably Hollywood, and Britain.

Like the frequent denunciations of British imperialism, which is often presented as English, and notably so by the Scots, the Welsh and, even more, the Irish, this last feature leads to a lack of engagement with the past for its own sake. This was one seen in the mid-2010s in a rise in demands for apologies for the past, demands already pressed from the 1990s. This absence of specificity, in the sense of an understanding of the circumstances of particular past periods, captures a key problem with British history as currently presented. Where it most attracts attention, it is frequently misconstrued, in a new version of the Whiggishness often decried by scholarly commentators. In practice, once great,

Britain had a more noble, and more distinctive, history than is often allowed for, but it is also a history that has been largely superseded by, and in, a very different age. That is the background to current discussion of nationalisms within Britain.

History, nevertheless, is an important approach to the understanding of English nationalism, however defined and dated. This is not only because nationalism developed in the past. It is also because English nationalism very much looked to the past when presenting an account of national distinctiveness. Indeed, history, rather than ethnicity, was crucial to English nationalism. This nationalism was the product of historical events as encapsulated in constitutionalism and its presentation or collective memory. In 1784, the writer John Andrews argued that:

> An Englishman should be particularly versed in history, not only that of his own country, but those of as many others as he can possibly spare the time to read and study. It is chiefly by an application of this kind that he will become of public utility: he will learn what courses to avoid, by contemplating the calamities they have occasioned; and what measures to pursue, by considering the benefits they have produced. Men of rank and fortune in some other countries, may doubtless attain the same knowledge; but in them it will prove inactive and fruitless: it is only in states blessed with liberty that such a science is not a dead letter to the possessor. Study therefore history beyond all other subjects.[2]

Six years later, in response to the French Revolution, the *London Chronicle* of 2 March 1790 commented:

> The Frenchman acknowledged that they had been miserable and wretched, but pleased himself with the prospect of what was to come; he said that 'the States General ... were forming a constitution preferable in many respects to that of England ... that the Tiers Etat [Third Estate, bourgeoisie, the radical Estate].' Here the Englishman interrupted with 'D-n your Tiers Etat! Where is your Magna Carta and your Bill of Rights!'

INTRODUCTION

Another context to English nationalism was, and is, presented by that of localities, especially parishes, towns, and counties, in short the 'intermediate institutions' of nationhood. Their senses of identity, continuity and immediacy were important to that of the nation, and sufficiently so for the major changes in local government under the Local Government Act of 1972 to be a significant aspect of the decline of traditional patterns, not only of local identity but also of English nationalism. Scant consideration was given then to the value of traditional identities in providing a sense of place and belonging. These localities had been important across a range of activities, and resulting values and identities, including government, the military, the Church, and the state. Many continue to be relevant despite the 1972 legislation, and some of the measures were reversed or otherwise changed with subsequent legislation from 1986.

Continuity was that of a society that was reverential of the past, and reverential to it. This was an aspect of the role of family, the 'nationalism,' or rather identity, of which was expressed in lineage and social customs. Family names were an aspect of this. Christening was a religious act, and also a means of joining the new-born to an existing family. Individuality and family worked in fashions and contexts that were different from those of today. Whereas the choice of name today is often unrelated to lineage and, instead, may reflect names that are liked or associations with popular entertainment or sport, in the past names very much captured the weight of the past, secular and spiritual, family and national. Moreover, those who were long-lived were regarded as of particular merit, and the cults of the young and of modernity were less prominent than in modern society. Individual and collective memory were highly important. The law gave weight to the memory of old members of the community. Dynasticism was important at all levels. It included the retention of family correspondence as an aspect of history by heirloom. There was also the commissioning of portraits and the retention of those of previous members of families. A similar end was achieved by means of commissioning pictures of houses.

Much of the discussion about national identity tends to be about the role of men. This is inappropriate. Women wrote and read about aspects of identity, with history playing an important role. Samuel Johnson claimed over dinner on 29 April 1778 that 'all our ladies read now'. Women were also subjects for the discussion of identity and history.[3] Female activism could take many forms, including a Christian womanhood focused, outside the home, on charity and education. This was one account of the female contribution to nationhood and was supported for example by Hannah More (1745–1833), a prominent Evangelical writer.[4] Writers such as Elizabeth Carter (1717–1806) and Catherine Talbot (1721–70) presented women's religious commitment as a vital element in the moral progress of the country. They regarded religious orthodoxy as important in achieving their goal, and historical writing as part of a religious commitment. Women's piety and learning were regarded, moreover, by some as an element in cultural advancement.

There was also an emphasis on women as prominent figures in the nation's past. This appeared particularly appropriate given the idea of an elect nation and the extent to which women featured strongly in Biblical histories such as those re-enacted in Handel's oratorios. Boudica (Latinised as Boadicea), an opponent of Roman rule, was first among the female rulers whose martial virtues were emphasised. Elizabeth I was seen as a powerful woman who had changed the course of history. Somewhat implausibly, Queen Anne was praised in the same fashion. Between 1689 and 1740, Oxford saw two statues erected to Anne, as well as one each to Mary II, the wife of William III, and Caroline of Ansbach, the wife of George II.

A key issue was the extent to which women contributed to the progress of civilisation and the advance of England. The changing position of women was to be incorporated into a progressive view of national culture and destiny by being regarded as an aspect of Protestantism. Women's role in marriage was seen as an important element in the moral improvement of society and, notably, the refinement of men and the appropriate conduct of the clergy. Female historians, however, did not simply rest on the Reformation. Instead, the Anglo-Saxons, the Celts, and the chivalric medieval world were, separately and collectively, presented as transmitting to the present a powerful cultural ancestry in which women could enjoy high status and act as examples.

Discussion of the role of women serves as a reminder of the separate strands, settings, and sources of nationhood, and, therefore, of the need to move away from any single account of it. This is true of nationalism in the past, and therefore underlines the folly of any mono-dimensional account of it in the present. Indeed, from a variety of perspectives, there is a number of interesting and important recent discussions of Englishness.[5] None exhaust the topic, but they underline the extent to which English identity is not so much elusive as capable of different approaches. That is not a definition of elusiveness, but, instead, a reminder, alongside the overlapping, but not coterminous, character of Englishness, national identity, nationhood and nationalism, of the inherently contentious nature of identity. To pretend otherwise may be helpful politically, but it is inaccurate.

2

THE OLD ENGLISH STATE

England as a united state was a creation of the tenth century, as the ruling house of Wessex conquered the lands of the Angles in the Midlands, the North, and East Anglia, subjugating the Vikings, many of whom had been settled there for decades. This conquest led to a sense of identity that was to be recovered by subsequent interest in the period, including a cultural Anglo-Saxonism. The cohesion of the English state was readily apparent in the Middle Ages, after the abrupt dislocation created by the Norman Conquest of 1066, in large part because the Normans and, after them, the Angevins built on the Anglo-Saxon inheritance.

Focus on the Anglo-Saxon origins of the Old English state takes us back to the fifth-century Angle, Saxon and Jute invasions of Romanised Britain, which in practice was only part (albeit the preponderant part) of modern Britain. That focus also helps to provide a millennium-long or rather longer history for that of England. At the same time, this approach faces difficulties, not least because (as with the present) there were then alternative destinies for England, and at a more protean stage of history.

The two most significant alternative destinies, each of which indeed lasted for centuries, were, first, Roman Britain and, secondly, and covered in the next chapter, the Anglo-Norman monarchy. The first provided the original unification of England, which had earlier been divided among tribal kingdoms. That unification was achieved by means of a conquest that began in 43 CE (AD) and continued, in England, until the early 70s. Roman Britain included not only all of what became England, but also all of what became Wales and what became southern Scotland. Furthermore, Roman Britain was part of an empire, one ruled from Rome and directed to Roman purposes. Although citizenship was extended throughout the empire and, eventually, a form of devolved collective imperial leadership introduced to address challenges, there was no intention that this empire would become a federation of independent dominions prefiguring the course envisaged for the British Empire from the late nineteenth century. Nor did Roman Britain provide much for what became English identity or, indeed, 'deep history.' As such, it contrasted with the experience of Roman rule in France, Italy, and Spain, although it is not helpful to treat any as a coherent unit in this period.

There was in practice an important legacy from Roman Britain, but, in England, these proved less deep-rooted and more ephemeral, than in France, Italy, and Spain. At the same time, there were legacies, continuities as well as significant later echoes, at least to some extent, in urban life, Christianity, and aspects of *Romanitas* (Romanness) as to the extent to which English rulers saw England in relation to the *Sacrum Imperium Romanorum* (Holy Roman Empire) during the Middle Ages.

Although Rome acted as a model for later British imperialism, there was also to be a reaction against Rome when constructing accounts of Englishness. The latter owed much to ideas and, to a degree, practices of liberty and self-government, a combination that was not offered by Roman citizenship. To later critics, Rome represented foreign rule, slavery, and a paganism that was only partly countered by a conversion to what became, at least as seen from the sixteenth century, Roman Catholicism.

Similarly, there was a reaction against the Anglo-French monarchy that followed the Norman Conquest of 1066 and that lasted, in various forms, until the end of the Hundred Years' War in 1453. This monarchy was to be regarded as arising from the overthrow of the Old English state at the battle of Hastings in 1066; and English nationalism was to be seen as a reaction to, liberation from, and transformation of, this monarchy. Thus, the rise of Parliament and the vernacular became narratives of the revival of Englishness after a period of foreign rule, with the foreignness notably seen in un-English concepts and practices of law, governance, and culture.

A common theme was that of destructiveness, the pressures placed on the nation by conquest. This was a repeated process, one ascribed to the Romans, Saxons, Vikings and Normans. Thus, Sir Henry Chauncy's *Historical Antiquities of Hertfordshire* (1700) began:

> When the Saxons had subdued the Britons, and made themselves masters of this land, they endeavoured to extinguish the religion, laws, and language of the ancient inhabitants; therefore destroying all marks of antiquity that nothing might remain, which could discover to the people of future ages that any other but themselves were the first inhabitants of this country; they gave new names to all towns, villages, and other places.[1]

This was a death of history. In turn, Chauncy was highly critical of the harshness of Norman conquest. This approach exemplified anew the significance of independence to national identity, and thus to nationalism. Hostility to the 'Norman Yoke' provided a backdrop to the sixteenth-century and later treatment of the Protestant Reformation of that century. Chauncy was a lawyer which helps explain his assertion of the centrality of law and legal customs to an English identity.

There was much diversity in Anglo-Saxon England, including not only political difference in independent states, but also contrasts in the economy and in vernacular architecture. Mapping the various categories of data, both written and physical, as opposed to extrapolating from very fragmentary survivals to imagine the whole, as historians have always done, underlines the diversity of England. Linked to that, some areas had much in common with other parts of Britain or, indeed, Europe; for example an inhabitant of Gloucestershire had a degree of affinity with the nearby Welsh. Within England, west-east contrasts were as important as north-south ones, and this situation may have looked toward a more lasting one, still seen for example in late-medieval England. The high monastic culture imposed a uniform layer at the top social levels, but the situation at other levels was much more varied.[2]

An Anglo-Saxon culture has been discerned by the late sixth century, and a linguistically distinct *gens Anglorum* (English people) by the early eighth century. Collective Christian worship and common religious practice were important to the forging of identity.[3] The canons of the Synod of Hertford (672) were issued for, and applied to, the whole English Church. Bede, a Northumbrian monk, wrote his *Ecclesiastical History of the English People* in 731. His purpose was ecclesiastical, not political, but his view of the English kingdoms ensured that he became a 'founder' of English history.

At the same time, there was the coalescence of the numerous small kingdoms into three major kingdoms: Northumbria, Mercia and Wessex, in the North, Midlands and South respectively. It was difficult to perpetuate any hegemony amongst these, although, from at least king Aethelbert of Kent in the 590s (the ruler who received the missionary, St Augustine of Canterbury), there were attempts to act as a *bretwalda* (overking). In the seventh century, this position was grasped by kings of Northumbria. The kings of the different kingdoms were very closely related by marriage, while their households included retainers from other kingdoms such that England was united as a political and cultural society with a network including clerics, some of whom were of the royal blood. Thus the warfare was not between competing warlords.[4] After the defeat of Northumbria, Offa of Mercia (r. 757–96) used the term 'king of the English' at least once in his charters. He was also responsible for a more standardised silver penny, which became the basis of English currency. From 786 to 802, Wessex recognised Mercian protection.

It was under Alfred of Wessex (r. 871–99) that the reality and image of an English state and English nationalism gathered pace. Alfred's reign and those of his able successors, notably Edward the Elder (r. 899–924) and Athelstan (r. 924–39), were important in the development of an English identity. They defeated and drove back the Danes, conquering the Midlands and, with greater difficulty, the North of England. Military prowess was important and the new system was affirmed through fortification. Thus, Chester was fortified in 907; Hertford in 911; Tamworth in 913; Buckingham and Warwick in 914; Cambridge, Colchester, Derby and Huntingdon in 917; Nottingham and Stamford in 918; and Manchester in 919.

Athelstan, after his conquest of Northumbria in 927, started to call himself *rex Anglorum* (king of the English) and, for his coins, became the first Anglo-Saxon king to be shown wearing a crown. The long witness lists to his charters provide evidence of significant national assemblies that look towards the later creation of Parliament.

Eadred (r. 946–55) was also described as king of the English, while, in 973, Edgar (r. 959–75) was the first to be crowned as king of the English. The earlier destruction of the other Anglo-

Saxon ruling houses by the Danes allowed Alfred and his successors to be portrayed as English, rather than merely West Saxon
kings. However, in another light, rather as with Naples and
Italian unification in 1860, Mercia and the North were conquered by the House of Wessex as the compromises that had
been made with the Danes were overthrown.

Alfred, who was an active patron of a vibrant Court culture
that extolled his merits, presented himself as the champion of
Christianity and of all Anglo-Saxons against the pagan Danes.
He reformed the Church and issued laws in English. Alfred was
a crucial figure in the shift towards a new politics and a new
kingdom, the Old English kingdom. This was a state that did
not require, or have, precise ethnic or geographic borders. This
point is directly relevant to the modern claim by critics that
English nationalism is a form of racism, or is, even, primarily
racist. In practice, that claim ignores the extent to which English
nationalism has, from the start, been a matter of those who lived
in England. In the ninth century, this included those who could
be regarded as Saxons, Angles, Jutes, Vikings and Britons. So
also with the present situation: Englishness, like Britishness, is
not a matter of ethnicity.

The eroding of the distinction between Mercia and Wessex
was especially notable in the tenth-century development of the
Old English kingdom. Further from the centre of power in
Wessex, Northumbria retained a greater sense of difference, certainly until the late eleventh century. This is an important
source, although not the only one, for the separate cultural identity of 'the North.'

The crowning of Edgar was important to the formation of a
unified English nation, and indeed in many respects critical
changes took place during c. 940–80.[5] Possibly as a consequence
of the influence of Carolingian (the Frankish dynasty of
Charlemagne) ideology, specifically the idea of a Christian

empire, expressed by Jonas of Orléans and Hincmar of Reims, which influenced Athelstan and Edgar, tenth-century Wessex moved towards a notion of kingship different from that of the amalgam of kingdoms epitomised in the eighth century by Offa of Mercia. Offa was very much a *bretwalda* and controlled such formerly independent kingdoms as Essex, Lindsey (part of what became Lincolnshire), East Anglia, Kent and Sussex, as well as London. In contrast, the period from Alfred to Edgar was that of the definition of an English state, one that did not require, nor was constrained by, precise ethnic, tribal or geographical borders. The English state was a developed one. Going back to the late ninth century, the improvement of the coinage, with Alfred responsible for a new standard for the penny, indicated that this was not rule by warrior band and that the government had considerable sophistication.

The expanding state, and its linked nationalism, also developed internally, a process that helped it to become distinctive and that was assisted by England south of the Humber being relatively small.[6] Most significantly, there was the consolidation of a county or shire system, which provided a regular link between rulers and free men, and an effective means of assessment for taxation and military service. Indeed, freedom, as understood in the terms of a period in which there were slaves, was to be a key link in ideas about national character and identity. Freedom was a matter of positive group inclusion and of assertion against what might be construed as unreasonable. Being 'bloody-mindedly' independent toward authority is a definition of English national identity that has long been offered. In terms of rights, however claimed, this practice and definition long preceded the notion of representation in or via a Parliament, and was also more socially extensive and active than the other.

Thus, the law, both the rights it enshrined and the ability to enforce rights and resolve disputes in an acceptable fashion, rather than Parliament, was the key element. The defence of rights by the law was intended as a peaceful way to resolve disputes including between those of different ethnic and/or political backgrounds. Such a system of resolution protected both trade and the Church.

The Old English state was to be important not only to subsequent accounts of English history but also to the historical grounding of its British imperial counterpart. In their *Historical and Modern Atlas of the British Empire* (1905), C. Grant Robertson and J.G. Bartholomew, far from dating the empire to the late Tudor period of maritime expansion, saw a longer imperial destiny:

> Since the days of Boadicea there is no period of our history in which the inhabitants of Great Britain have not been connected with or lived under a series of national and historic imperial systems ... the theory and claims of the modern imperial crown are no pinchbeck [false metal] creation of the nineteenth century.

The long procession of earlier imperial episodes gave modern British imperialism a legitimating history, one that made it appear natural. The earlier episodes, according to the authors, were not an 'irrelevant' prologue, but rather 'continuously and organically connected' with modern British imperialism. One map was entitled 'Empire of Wessex'.[7]

At the same time, there is controversy over the nature, power, and stability of the Old English state. An emphasis on Old English strength[8] and institutional sophistication suggests that the origins of modern England can be located in this state. This is a view that encourages a stress on the longevity of England and on its institutional origins in the participatory system of Old English public courts and governance. Conversely, it is also possible to question both points, not least by querying the power of the Old English state in northern England and, more generally, the extent to which it did more than overawe contrary tendencies. The intensive lordship shown by the Crown in Wessex and south Mercia can be contrasted with an extensive lordship elsewhere into the late tenth century.[9]

Although Old English statehood was a far-flung kingship that covered essentially the area of modern England, it is unclear how far this led to a concept of Englishness and the English nation as matching these bounds. The political language of the Old English state certainly served to include peoples of differing ethnic background who, in addition, had been under independent rulers. The language of national sentiment can be seen in the poem that commemorated the honourable defeat by the Danes at Maldon in 991, as well as with the treatment of some saints as national figures. The extent to which these views were widely held is unclear. So also was the position in border areas.

Nevertheless, this point is true of most historical periods. Moreover, and this argument is highly relevant for the consideration of the present-day situation, and, indeed, the contentiousness over Brexit, the idea of any national identity without qualification or contradiction, is far-fetched. By the standards of the age, the Old English monarchy ruled what was an effective and powerful state. As a result, the political, constitutional, and governmental history of England can be readily traced to the ninth century. Effective royal justice, combined with a system of lawcourts, were important to the development of English law, then and in the long term. 'Common Law,' which was to be a vital element of English nationalism, in essence suggested common values policed by the courts.

Despite the political crises and territorial divisions of the period, the powerful administration, including a form of national taxation, introduced by the West Saxon dynasty into much of modern England, did develop a sense of national consciousness. The term Anglo-Saxon was increasingly used in late ninth-century royal charters. The term *rex Anglorum* was employed on coins. The extent to which England was a state was seen in the way in which it could be taken over as a unit in 1016 by Cnut of Denmark and in 1066 by William of Normandy, in each case as a result of war followed by submission. Unlike earlier invaders, culminating in the Vikings in the ninth century, each seized a kingdom of England.

This kingdom did not have precise borders. Indeed, in the tenth century, the kingdom of the Scots overran Strathclyde, Lothian and Cumbria, a process aided by the degree to which there was no obvious geographical boundary between Scotland and England, and no ethnic unity to either. Indeed, what eventually became Scotland included Scots, Picts, Angles, and Britons, and, until the mid-twelfth century, it was unclear whether Cumbria and Northumbria would be part of England or of Scotland. That the kings of Scotland were to owe fealty and homage to the kings of England for lands they held in northern England subsequently complicated the situation. Scotland did not abandon the northern counties until the Quitclaim, or Treaty, of York in 1237.

The political character of England and Scotland emerges more clearly by considering Wales. It is unclear whether Gwynedd, the principality in north-west Wales, could have developed as Wessex did in the tenth and eleventh centuries, serving as the basis for a Welsh state, but, unlike England, there is little sign of governmental sophistication in Wales, and less than there was in Scotland. The 'conquest' of one part of Wales, Ireland, and, even Scotland, by the ruler of another amounted to a personal submission and the giving of hostages, rather than administrative control and consolidation. However, in all parts of the British Isles, military success was a key element.

With its growing pretensions to overlordship in Britain, the English state came to intervene more in Scotland and, far more, Wales. The South Welsh in 886 made some kind of submission to

Alfred, to whom they turned for help against the Vikings, and this may have lasted into the early tenth century. Welsh rulers attended Athelstan's court and were regarded by him as subordinates.

The politics of eleventh-century England included several conflicts over the succession, conflicts that could be seen in nationalist or proto-nationalist terms. Thus, after Edward the Confessor (r. 1042–66) came to the throne, restoring the 'Old English' dynasty, in the person of Aethelred the Unready's son, his favour for Normans, such as Robert of Jumièges, whom he made Archbishop of Canterbury in 1051, exacerbated Edward's poor relations with his powerful father-in-law, Earl Godwin of Wessex. The latter's success, at the head of an army, in obliging Edward to return him to favour in 1052 was followed by the expulsion of leading Normans, including Robert. This has been, and can be seen, in 'nationalist' terms. The *Anglo-Saxon Chronicle* gives the impression that Edward's Norman favourites were disliked because they were Normans, and does appear to reflect a degree of English nationalism, especially in explaining why, in the repeated crises of 1051–2, the two sides did not come to blows.

However, given Godwin's own history as a loyal supporter of the Danish rulers Cnut (r. 1016–35) and his son Harold Harefoot (r. 1035–40), nationalist distinctions and terms must be employed with caution. Instead, as with clashes in the medieval period about the 'foreign' favourites of such monarchs as Henry III (r. 1216–72) and Edward II (r. 1307–27), it is also pertinent to stress the question of patronage, namely the access to the monarch that was crucial in aristocratic society. 'Foreignness' was then as much a question of response to being an unwelcome newcomer to the charmed circle, as a specific dissatisfaction with his place of origin. Godwin himself spent the winter of 1051–2 at Bruges under the protection of Count Baldwin of Flanders, while certain French favourites of Edward the Confessor who were deemed not to be a threat were permitted to stay after the expulsion of the others. Under Edward, the royal titles of king of the English and of the British were used interchangeably. And with reason: although Ireland was completely independent, Wales and Scotland were in part dependant.

Nationalism is frequently discussed as a product of the last quarter-millennium, not least with the argument that the sense of collective identity that existed within the framework of the monarchical state took a different form from that to be found in the nineteenth-century nation-state.[10] However, many of the characteristics of nationalism, including a collective name, shared history, a distinctive shared culture, an association with a specific territory, and a sense of solidarity, can be seen earlier,[11] and certainly so with England. Successive invasions meant that there was division within England as well as the sharing of circumstances, but the political cohesion created in the tenth century ensured that unity under the leadership of the Old English state was the key character. This unity was an important element of England as part of what was a heterogeneous 'outer Europe.'[12] That situation might not amount to English exceptionalism, but it was an important aspect of England's difference. Moreover, England was poised autonomously between the Frankish and Scandinavian worlds,[13] and, in part, developed accordingly.

3

LINKED TO FRANCE, 1066–1453

Norman conquest in 1066 was followed by a marked degree of Normanisation in Church and state, as well as with the imposition of a comprehensive feudalism and the commitment of England, now part of a more wide-ranging polity, to Continental power-politics. The ninth-century Danes had killed clerics, but not taken over the Church, which had thus remained the centre of English culture and consciousness. The Norman Conquest was far more pronounced. The cultural transformation of the Church was symbolised by the withering away of writing in English: the last version of the *Anglo-Saxon Chronicle*, still written up intermittently at Peterborough Abbey after the Conquest, ceased in the mid-twelfth century.

Yet, William I (r. 1066–87), who claimed to be Edward the Confessor's rightful successor, may not initially have intended to introduce sweeping changes, for Englishmen who submitted at the beginning of his reign were allowed to keep their lands. The surviving English earls were left in power. However, the scale and geographical extent of English resistance in 1068–70 to the consolidation of Norman rule led to the adoption by William of a harsher attitude. The English earls were removed by 1076. Moreover, the majority of English landowners came in time to be dispossessed, as *Domesday Book* (1086) reveals. After the many deaths in the battles of 1066, many landowners were children and they were married off to Norman-French young men and women.

The English were generally treated as a conquered people and were turned into one remarkably fast. Although there was assimilation, not least through intermarriage, there was no comparison with the Roman attempt to co-opt and Romanise local elites: the Normans were too land-hungry and they had a different ethos and practice from that of the Romans.

Under Norman rule, there was a degree of continuity with the Old English state, particularly in the system of shires and of sheriffs as dismissable royal officials. Old institutions, however, were used for the benefit of new rulers with their own ideas of justice and government, and with novel problems. In particular, there was the defence of Normandy against its neighbours, principally the kingdom of France, and, in time, of England from rival Norman princes, in the rivalry between William I's sons. At the senior levels, the institutions were also staffed by different people, while the personal 'feudal' links of obligation that bound the Normans together differed in character from earlier social relationships in England. Anglo-Saxon ealdormen and thanes swore oaths of loyalty to the king and were expected to perform military service; and could lose their land for failure to perform military service. There were doubtless similarities between their position and that of Norman aristocrats, but the system of knight-service was novel. Under it, Norman magnates held their lands upon a military tenancy, obliging them to provide a number of knights that corresponded to the value of their estates.

There was also a replacement of English abbots and bishops, as well as a reorganisation of the diocesan system with some sees transferred, notably that of Dorchester-on-Thames to Lincoln. Norman ecclesiastics were sometimes uneasy about the cults associated with their new monastic houses, especially about English saints unknown beyond their own localities, for whom little written evidence, in the form of saints' lives, was available. Paul of Caen, Abbot of St Albans from 1077 to 1093, was accused of slighting the tombs of his predecessors, whom he referred to as uneducated simpletons, but he did not eject the relics of the saints of St Albans from the church. Relics were sometimes tested by fire, as at Evesham, although those which survived the test, as, in this instance, the relics of St Ecquine, were reinstated in new shrines. This unease was itself part of a wider Christian suspicion about saints whose existence was obscure and undocumented. As so often, it is necessary to put English developments in a broader context.

Similarly, institutional developments, such as the spread of new monastic orders, particularly the Austin Canons and the Cistercians, can be seen as 'foreign.' However, they also reflected the widespread movement for Church reform that characterised the late eleventh century. The international reform impulse in the Church, linked in particular to Pope Gregory VII (r. 1073–85), led to attempts to enforce clerical celibacy and to end the clerical dynasties that had become important among the parochial clergy. In addition, lay ownership of churches declined. Resistance to the Norman prelates owed something to opposition to a more general movement for reform, while their policies should be seen in the context of reform as much as of control.

In the twelfth century, a sense of Anglo-Norman identity and continuity was consciously developed, with Englishness and Britishness now being seen not in a negative light, but, rather, as memorable bases for a glorious present. The historical perspective was in large part constructed by clerics who had personal links with Anglo-Saxon England. The cult of saints, like the emphasis on monastic and ecclesiastical history, necessarily looked to the Anglo-Saxon past. In the work of Geoffrey of Monmouth (d. c. 1155), Anglo-Norman England latched on to a British past, as his *Historia Regum Britanniae* (c. 1136) traced events from the legendary founding of Britain by Aeneas of Troy's grandson, Brutus, and greatly developed the Arthurian legend: Arthur's father was now said to be a descendant of Constantine, and a conqueror of the French and the Romans. By the early eleventh century, a measure of celebration of the pre-Norman past was in order. However, the position had been very different in the aftermath of the Conquest. It was only once Norman rule was established that the focus could shift to adaptability and continuity.

In the twelfth century, there was a desire to preserve the laws truly or fictionally associated with Edward the Confessor, a process aided by the progressive enhancement of his reputation. Edward had issued a writ confirming the laws and jurisdiction of the London guild of *cnihtas* (males of high rank), and this writ was placed on the altar of the London priory of Holy Trinity, Aldgate, as confirmation of the guild's gift of land and rights. The London 'commune' of 1141, in which citizens and barons joined, asked Matilda for permission to live under the laws of Edward rather than those of her father Henry I (r. 1100–35), which were harsher, but she refused, which consolidated London's support for her eventually-successful rival, his nephew, king Stephen (r. 1135–54). The 1191 'commune' which advanced claims for London's interests brought together Londoners of English and Norman ancestry. Thus, a key element of the city's identity was that it took precedence over differences in ancestry and lineage, and, in doing so, brought otherwise distinct groups into a commonalty of shared identity and interests.

Similarly, buildings begun between 1066 and 1100 displayed distinctly Norman features, while few of the Anglo-Saxon deco-

rative traditions were continued or Anglo-Saxon-style manu-
scripts produced. The situation changed after 1100 with the
revival of Anglo-Saxon workshops and styles, and the creation of
a vibrant Anglo-Norman style. The latter was not nationalism,
but was related to a national distinctiveness that looked in that
direction. Separately, the English language continued, with most
of the English speaking it, even if the situation was different
within writing.

Although ruled within the trans-Channel polity established
by the Norman Conquest, and sustained by the eventual defeat
by Henry I of William I's attempt to divide his inheritance
among his sons, there were governmental developments in
England that were to be important to its later distinctive character. In particular, under Henry II (r. 1154–89), the first of the
Angevin dynasty, who ruled a more far-flung empire than that
of the Normans, extending as it did eventually into south-west
France and also Ireland, government in England necessarily
became less dependent on the personal intervention of the monarch. Henry did not try to develop a single cohesive governmental system. Instead, he expected to divide among his sons the
large group of lordships he had accumulated. Henry's successors,
however, saw themselves not simply as kings of England, but as
rulers of, or claimants to, the wider inheritance of Henry and, in
time, to the French throne.

After the civil war under Stephen and in response to the new
situation under Henry II, the administrative development of the
Old English state was resumed. Government remained public to
a far greater extent than in France. While France was little more
than a confederacy of princely courts, for example that of
Normandy, with that of the king the first among equals, England
had not fragmented. Instead, law brought the central government
and the localities closer together. Although bureaucratic practices
of government took a while to develop, these practices became

more fixed and significant. The new governmental structures of the sixteenth century, the period of the so-called 'Tudor Revolution in Government,' mostly of the 1530s, in fact looked back to the Middle Ages, and, in many senses, were another version of earlier developments.

War had a range of consequences, including the need to raise taxation. The French conquest of Normandy in 1203–4, with Philip Augustus of France replacing king John, was important in changing the relationship with the surviving Continental possessions of the kings of England, not least in underlining their vulnerability to French attack and ensuring that the intermediary possession of Normandy was no more. The former Anglo-Norman nobility were also obliged to choose whether to give allegiance to the king of England or to the king of France.

The French invasion of England in the following decade fostered anti-Frenchness; English victories at Dover and Sandwich in 1217 stimulated English pride. For that generation, these victories were of great significance, but now they are largely forgotten.

Alongside the political account, there is one of English society as particularly distinctive. The linkage between the two accounts is clearly that of the law, but legal practice was an expression of social behaviour alongside the state. The theme of England (not Britain) as distinctive, and of this distinctiveness as lasting, has been argued by a number of influential scholars, and with reference to much of the period. Thus, in 1992, Chris Wickham wrote:

> the hierarchies of free society are likely to have been less clearly structured in England than on the Continent... there may well have been rather less hierarchy, and certainly a less structured hierarchy, in pre-tenth-century England than in the Carolingian world.[1]

Offering an account of national exceptionalism, Alan Macfarlane argued that English society became distinctly, and distinctively, less stratified:

England has been inhabited since at least the thirteenth century by a people whose social, economic, and legal system was in essence different not only from that of peoples in Asia and Eastern Europe, but also in all probability from the Celtic and Continental countries of the same period ... [This was] not merely a matter of geography and language, but was rooted deep in its laws, customs and kinship system.[2]

At the same time as legal factors, environmental and technological constraints and possibilities were significant. In eastern England, but also in the Low Countries and northern Italy, convertible husbandry (switching from arable to pastoral) spread, helping to improve soil fertility and bringing more intensive arable farming. Such changes could work in two contrasting fashions, either accentuating differences between England (or parts of England) and other countries, or, as a consequence of the diffusion of techniques, minimising them. Each process played a part, but the second appears to have reduced differences between parts of England. Indeed, a stress on regional diversity within England is not an answer to the question of national distinctiveness. England in particular moved rapidly away from 'classical' feudalism and towards a money economy. By 1130, rents paid in money, rather than in goods and services, were very common on royal manors and other large estates in England. The dynamic nature of this economy was helped by the character of the law and by the presence of state authority.

The law developed especially from the twelfth century, into a system of Common Law that was distinctive both in the content of the law and in the way in which it was administered. The legal system reflected the particular imprint of international monarchs, especially Henry II and Edward I, and the nature of what was, by contemporary standards, a sophisticated administrative system that owed much to the strength of Norman and Angevin monarchical power. English Common Law had links with what was going on abroad, but was also a distinctive unity, and that at a time when Roman Law was coming back into fashion on the Continent and *later* in Scotland. Medieval Scots Law was much closer to English Common Law, although there were different institutional structures in Scotland with no central courts like the King's Bench and Common Pleas. Focused on precedent, Common Law was especially suited to the protection of rights and liberties, and encouraged a respect for the autonomy of individual thought and action. In combination with the early emergence of an institutional monarchy, this was responsible for the character and continuity of English political society.

The Common Law gained in strength, helping to consolidate England as a remarkably homogenous state by European standards. The character and role of the law served as a way to enhance public power, and contributed greatly to the extent to which England, in comparative terms, was much governed. Lords exercised much of their influence through the public courts system of hundred and shire that was a crucial inheritance from the Old English state; rather than through private judicial power. This was an important source of political, geographical, and social cohesion, and helped to ensure that influence over the government, rather than defiance of it, was the key dynamic of politics.[3] As a reminder of the difficulty of using modern terminology, this can be discussed in terms of avoiding the 'privatisation' of authority, of 'nationalising' power, and of not relying on the 'pillars of the community'. None of those phrases, however, is really pertinent or helpful. That defiance was a matter of opposition at the national level, rather than resistance at a regional one, was significant for the constitutional and political development of England in the short and long terms.

The 'rule of law' ensured a distinction between the Crown as a benign presence and the individual king as possibly arbitrary. The politics of the period left an event and document that were to be significant, indeed emblematic, for the later account of

Englishness and that was to be translated into the British historical tradition. What was later to be called Magna Carta, a charter
of liberties of 1215, was a wide-ranging condemnation of king
John's use of feudal, judicial, and other governmental powers, a
condemnation that defined and limited royal rights. Magna Carta
was in effect an enormous list of everything that was wrong with
government as John had applied it, notably arbitrary royal action.
This agreement forced from the king by baronial opponents, was
a limitation in written form of royal rights. It thereby came to be
seen as a charter of liberties and a rejection of the 'Norman
Yoke.' Moreover, Magna Carta had a long and lasting resonance.
It came to play a key role in a narrative of the nation and was
thus occasion and process, event and symbol.

By creating a new relationship between the king and the law
that was in effect England's first written constitution, Magna
Carta asserted the importance of placing royal power under the
law, and freemen were provided with some guarantees against
arbitrary royal action. Magna Carta was to acquire totemic significance, being cited by opponents of what was presented as
arbitrary government power. The Common Lawyers, such as Sir
Edward Coke (1552–1634), Chief Justice of the King's Bench
(1613–16) and author of the *Institutes of the Laws of England*,
who had played the leading role in discovering a new political
role for Magna Carta in the early seventeenth century, were
heavily involved in drafting the charters of the English colonies
established in North America. The rejection of George III in
1775–83 by many of the North American colonists was regarded
as another instance of the opposition to king John and thus a
rejection of unwarranted royal power.

The hostility to the 'Norman Yoke' was also very much seen
in the later treatment of Magna Carta, a treatment which provided a lasting basis for an assertion of Englishness. This was not
only a question of the seventeenth and eighteenth centuries.

Echoes are still offered. A poll conducted for the *BBC History Magazine*, and reported in its June 2006 issue, offered a choice of ten days for 'On what historical day do you think Britain should celebrate British Day?,' and elicited the highest response for Magna Carta Day, 15 June. On 12 March 2014, Tim Berners-Lee, speaking on BBC Radio Four, called for a 'Magna Carta-like Charter of Rights' to guarantee rights on the web. Also in 2014, at a time of concern over alleged Islamic penetration of secondary education, David Cameron, the Prime Minister, ordered that every school pupil be taught the 'British values' enshrined in Magna Carta, adding that its principles 'paved the way for the democracy, the equality, the respect, and the laws that make Britain, Britain,' and that he would make the 800th anniversary the centrepiece of a fightback against extremism. It is as if, however, Magna Carta was a foundation document, and has become a substitute for a written constitution.

In practice, this charter of 1215, with its criticisms of the rule of John and its affirmation of a different standard of governance, was more directly English than a matter of Scottish or Welsh history. John ruled England, part of Wales, a smaller section of Ireland, and a decreasing number of French dominions, but he never ruled Scotland or all of Wales or Ireland.

Parliament was not mentioned in Magna Carta, and indeed not until the 1230s. However, Magna Carta was in practice an important stage in the development of Parliament, notably with clauses twelve and fourteen linking taxation to consent. Parliament turned out to be a pathway to constitutional government that was more effective than the issuing of charters by a monarch. Under Henry III (r. 1216–72), shire knights began to be elected to Parliament and, from 1265, selected towns sent representatives. The new concept of representation was outlined in the writs summoning representatives of the clergy, counties, and boroughs to the 1295 Parliament, which was held by Edward

I (r. 1272–1307), who, in many respects, was as important as Henry VIII was to be for the constitutional development of England. The representatives were instructed to appear with authority to give advice and consent on behalf of the communities they spoke for. The Commons filled up with local folk who supported the Common Law.

The development of Parliament was a matter not only of raising taxation, but also of the more general need for a political body that would serve, however episodically, as a national political focus, and thus as a means of, and for, nationalism in the broadest sense. This need was the product of the greater appeal of the national sense of political identity. The development of Parliament, which was part, and an increasingly significant part, of the delicate political compact necessary for peace and stability, entailed the broadening out of what had originated as the king's council of barons.

Politics was also very much involved in England's position within the international Church. This was seen in Henry II's ultimately violent dispute with Thomas Becket, Archbishop of Canterbury, from 1162 to 1170, and in the interdict on England imposed by Pope Innocent III in 1208: all Church services were suspended as part of the more general response to king John's policies. In the fourteenth century, Papal power in England was at its height, but there had for long been considerable hostility to Papal taxation, and it was a great issue in the early thirteenth century, a period of growing sensitivity about 'foreign' demands on English resources. In 1226, a Papal demand that a prebend should be assigned to the Pope in every non-monastic cathedral in England was rejected. Such demands for funds and patronage led to growing antagonism, so that in the 1230s there was a considerable display of hostility to foreign elements in the Church. This led to attacks on tithe barns owned by alien priories: priories whose mother houses were foreign monasteries, such as Cluny. There was a widespread movement in 1231 against alien absentees, especially Italians, who had been presented by the Pope to English benefices. Edward I was also determined to limit the Papal prerogative, and this broadened out into a general hostility to foreign ecclesiastical jurisdiction and to the related movement of funds abroad.

This opposition has to be located carefully in the consideration of the identity and expression of nationalism. It was part of a more widespread antagonism throughout society to strangers, to everyone who was not known. This ensured that 'foreigners' included 'internal' outsiders: people from other settlements or regions. This was an aspect of the gradual coalescence into communities. This coalescence entailed the more settled and defined settlements and borders, whether physical, legal, political, or mental, at every level, that were crucial in the growing definition of parochialism, regionalism, and nationalism. As earlier toward the Vikings, there was hostility to Jews, Italians, Flemings, the French, the Welsh, the Irish, and the Scots. Nationalism has always been in part a matter of definition and defence against outsiders.

That approach might sound mechanistic, and, separately, unattractive. At the same time, this definition of nationalism captures what has been more recently referred to as the tension between 'somewhere' and 'anywhere,' in short those with an identity linked with a particular location and those who do not have one.[4] The former may be of different ethnic backgrounds but define themselves with regard to the area they inhabit and thus constitute a nationhood based on place. In turn, that can lead to hostility to 'internal' outsiders, however defined.

In the political and religious spheres, the reign of Henry III was of particular significance. Boniface of Savoy, Archbishop of Canterbury 1243–70, the uncle of Henry's wife, made himself unpopular with his apparent hostility to national interests, although, in 1257–8, he rode the tide by organising meetings of the English bishops to oppose the claims of the Papal *nuncio* (representative). Henry became unpopular as a result of his favour for 'foreign' advisors, although many, especially his Poitevin half-brothers of the House of Lusignan, were subjects from his French possessions. This highlighted the English identification of outsiders as a process that was hostile to the Crown and also rested on a sense of Englishness. Under John and Henry III, the English nobility displayed a growing reluctance to commit to the defence of the king's French possessions, a situation that underlined the later skill of Edward III (r. 1327–77) in winning such support.

One prominent favourite, Simon de Montfort, was made Earl of Leicester by Henry III, but the Earl and King fell out, and Simon became the leader of an English baronial movement that was determined to limit royal powers and was opposed to Henry's 'foreign' favourites. In 1258, hostility to aliens played a crucial role in an attempt, in the document known as the Provisions of Oxford, to limit royal authority. As aspects of the movement many foreigners were expelled and royal castles were mostly entrusted to Englishmen. In 1263, there was a renewed burst of anti-alien and anti-Crown authority, in part a response to the deployment of foreign mercenaries. Hostility to aliens, especially their exclusion from office, was a crucial theme in the ultimately unsuccessful baronial struggle with Henry in 1264–5. Political society was Anglicised even if the monarchy was still Anglo-French.

War with France and Scotland from the 1290s played an important role in the constitutional and cultural fixing of a sense of identity. Taxes were justified as being for the 'common good'. This was part of a long pattern in English, later British, history in which the need for taxation was traded against the demand for redress of grievances and for the entrenching of individual liberty. As a result, the constitution and the establishment of rights became a matter of the assertion of parliamentary sovereignty, and not basic law, as in many other states. The emphasis on the sovereignty of Parliament, a body that, crucially, could revise its decisions, ensured that the constitution was regarded as incremental and seamless, and, despite the reputation of Magna Carta, not based on a founding document as it was to be in America. Parliament was an important English element in the wider process by which communities were in part defined by the developing governmental structures of the period, especially the administration of the law.[5]

Parliament also underlined a growing geographical fixedness that was to be important to the definition and configuration of English nationalism. There was representation from specific places to a body that legislated for a particular area. This was not, however, the sole aspect of fixedness. The modern concept of a specific capital would not have been recognised in the twelfth century, a situation which was linked to the slow erosion in the status of Winchester and the gradual rise of London's governmental position, while York retained an important *de facto* role as a northern capital as late as the seventeenth century. Edward I, Edward II, Edward III, and Richard II, at times moved the centre of government northward when war with Scotland made this convenient, as from 1298 to 1304 for Edward I. Parliament could meet outside London, but a general settling down of Parliament in Westminster gathered pace in the second half of the fifteenth century.

Nationalism, and the sense of national identity on which it rested, were encouraged not only by the development of Parliament, but also in accounts of history. The Norman monarchs sought to claim the historical inheritance of Old English kingship, in part by their support of religious foundations linked to this kingship. This process was taken forward by the sponsorship of historical writing. Later kings, especially Henry III and Edward III, very much supported such activity and added fresh initiatives of their own. Edward used the Arthurian legend to provide the authority of age for his embrace of chivalric ideals. This was seen with the establishment of the Order of the Garter in 1348–9 and the foundation of the College of St George to serve the royal chapel in Windsor Castle. This chapel was re-dedicated to St George whom Edward chose as the patron saint for the Order. This linkage of saint and nation was intended to bring prestige and success, and thus provided a form of white magic for nationalism, one that certainly still resonated for some at wartime in the twentieth century.

On a pattern also seen elsewhere in Europe, legislation in the fourteenth century was designed to establish limits on the rights of the Papacy. The Statute of Carlisle of 1307 forbade English and foreign clerics from taking money out of the realm. The Statutes of Provisors (1351, reissued 1390) and Praemunire (1353, extended 1393) theoretically prevented provisions to benefices by the Pope and appeals to him in lawsuits. All these statutes were enforced in a decidedly episodic and irregular way, but they were potent weapons that could be used. In 1414, under Henry V (r. 1413–22), an Act of Parliament confiscated the alien priories, thus asserting national interests and making the transfer of funds to international religious orders more difficult. The assertiveness of rulers and Parliaments that sought greater power over the Church in their dominions was an aspect of a proto-nationalism that was linked to ideas of distinctive character as well as rights, and that drew on a conviction that nations had a continuity that conveyed these rights. The dynastic theme remained significant, but also broadened out with a greater emphasis on place and people. A pre-Reformation 'national' church was crystalising. Henry VI (r. 1422–61, 1470–1) sought to have Alfred canonised, while the fastest growing cult in early Tudor England was that of Henry VI, to whom miracles were attributed and who was informally regarded as a saint and martyr.

A stress on proto-nationalism, Parliament and national politics provides a modern tone to this period, one particularly characterised by ideas and terms of development and progress. This approach captures an important aspect of change. It also underplays other themes, mostly the role of the Church, which very much represented an international identity, one accentuated by the increased power of the Papacy from the late eleventh century, and more particularly from the early thirteenth. A particular aspect of national identity, that of ethnic and religious exclusion, was provided by the expulsion of England's Jewish community by Edward I in 1290.

A significant cultural development that does look modern was provided by the rise of vernacular usage, which represented a rejection of the French-speaking culture that had arrived with the Norman Conquest. The role of Latin and of Anglo-Norman or Norman-French (the French spoken in England) declined. The Conquest brought in a French-speaking élite, and it was probably not until the late fourteenth century that English became an acceptable language in upper-class circles, although that is not easy to assess. The use of French declined from the early twelfth century, but it became fashionable again, more than ever before, in the thirteenth century.

After the Norman Conquest, Latin took over in the law and Church which had, since Alfred, used the vernacular which the Normans did not understand. Latin replaced English in official documents in the 1070s. Latin was also the language used by William for his documents as Duke of Normandy. A trilingual situation was to be the case in England for more than 200 years in which high language functions were divided between French and Latin. In the twelfth, thirteenth, and early-fourteenth centuries, the coronation oath was taken in French, so that it would be understood by all present. The Latin versions kept in the official recensions were simply a matter of record. Coronation records for the fourteenth and fifteenth centuries are sparse, but it is probable that the practice of giving and taking the oath in French continued. Anglo-Norman, however, was by the thirteenth century not the same language as that used in France: accent, grammar and vocabulary were all different, although there was no real communication problem, and there were also important variations within France itself as well as different languages such as Occitan in Languedoc.

The English language, which was moulded in the South-East, was increasingly identified with an English people and nation in the thirteenth century. Works written in English included the anonymous *Gawain and the Green Knight* (late fourteenth century), Geoffrey Chaucer's *Canterbury Tales* (c. 1387), William Langland's *Piers Plowman* (different versions, 1362–92), and Thomas Malory's *Morte d'Arthur* (1469), as well as ballads, carols, and mystery plays. The vernacular could be an expression and source of national consciousness, and was crucial to both. Laurence Minot (c.1300–c.1352) used English for his vigorous poetry of the 1330s and 1340s, with its stress on the unity of the English in their triumphs over the French and the Scots: xenophobic accounts of the battles of Crécy, Halidon Hill, Neville's Cross, and other victories. Aggressive feelings of identity were focused by conflict. It also served to bring ancestry myths into the present, and to develop symbols of collective identity, such as St George, who became a national saint in England, although also venerated elsewhere.[6]

War helped to create, sustain and broaden a sense of 'us' and 'them'. In 1344, parliamentary proceedings recorded Edward III's claim that Philip VI of France was 'firmly resolved ... to destroy the English nation and occupy the land of England.'[7] During the Hundred Years' War, a soldier's cry was either St George or St Denis.

The vernacular, however, could also serve for the transmission of cosmopolitan ideas and an international consciousness.

Moreover, it is far from clear that specific medieval artistic styles, such as the Perpendicular, had any political reverberations or any relationship with proto-nationalism. English culture was still part of a wider Western European cultural world.

Within England, vernacular usage, which was encouraged by the adoption of English by government agencies, such as the proceedings in the London Sheriffs' courts in 1356, and by the rise of mercantile groups, offered a degree of social unity that could ensure political action across social divides.[8] Lollardy, a late fourteenth century movement that challenged the position of the Pope and emphasised the authority of the Bible, favoured an English Bible. The use of English in its standard form was a fourteenth- and fifteenth-century development that was to be pushed further under the Tudors (1485–1603), when it became the language of authority and of culture.

At the same time, there was a strong, contrary drive to maintain a role in France. Henry V sought to revive the strongly-pressed claim of his great-grandfather, Edward III, to the French throne. Neither had any sense that the English Channel should act as a boundary to their authority. Although identifying with the cult of St George, and presented essentially as an exponent of Englishness in Shakespeare's play *Henry V* (1599), the king himself followed all his predecessors since William the Conqueror in envisaging a realm that spanned the English Channel. Normandy appeared closer to his centre of power in southern England than the margins of his possessions in the British Isles, and France, with its wealth and reputation, was also a more attractive and honourable prospect for operations and expansion.

Defeated by Henry, most famously at Agincourt (1415), a battle that was greatly to resonate with Shakespeare and thus to be employed in a famous film version during the Second World War, Charles VI of France betrothed his daughter, Catherine, to Henry, and, by the Treaty of Troyes of 1420, recognised Henry (and his heirs) as his heirs. Had Henry V lived longer, he might have created a new polity that probably would have left English nationalism as a reaction against the Crown. Instead, Henry died, probably of dysentery, in 1422, leaving an heir less than one year old. By 1453, the French had driven the English out of all bar Calais, which was not recaptured by France until 1558.

The claim to the French throne was only abandoned in the reign of George III (1760–1820), by the Treaty of Amiens (1802); while the Channel Isles, the last of the Norman legacy, are still held by the Crown. However, France was lost. There were to be further invasions of France, by Edward IV, Henry VII, and Henry VIII, but the failure of these rulers to achieve their ambitions in France was important to the development of English nationhood and government, and helped to underline an insular character to Britain's subsequent European identity. This character has been contested by some historians, but it was certainly more pronounced than the situation earlier in the Middle Ages. Moreover, in some respects, the Hundred Years' War itself offered a cultural precursor to the Protestant Reformation of the sixteenth century. At the start of the war, the aristocracy of England was international in outlook but, as politics drove the two realms into a long war, so it became awkward that high society in England aped French style, manners, and customs.

There is the more general point that the end of the Hundred Years' War and the Reformation, events that occurred within a century of each other, represented a breaking away from existing links with Europe. They also led to the altering of other links, or the creation of new ones, as with other Protestant powers. Whether it is helpful to make comparisons with recent or current changes is unclear. Everything is specific to itself and its context, and diachronic comparisons, those across time, can appear particularly suspect. At the same time, when considering abrupt changes, it is frequently helpful to turn to other periods of transformation. From that perspective, the period from 1453 is notable as leading to an enforced insularity that also saw England as greatly affected by the policies of other powers, mostly France and Burgundy during the Wars of the Roses (and related later conspiracies) from the 1450s to the 1490s, and France and Spain during the Reformation. Furthermore, failure in the Hundred Years' War and, later, the Reformation were each followed by conflict within England.

The government also manipulated patriotic characteristics and, in doing so, deliberately harnessed linguistic awareness. The earliest parliamentary petition in England was in 1386. Henry V himself switched to English in 1417, a significant year given the intensity then of the war with France. From 1420, Chancery clerks were pushing English as the official language of government. London's Guild of Brewers followed two years later. The degree to which this was 'nationalism' can be debated; but there was certainly the pursuit of a strong element of distinctiveness.

Foreign wars, and the expansion of royal authority in England, encouraged a focus, supportive and critical, on the pretensions, power, personnel, and policies of central government; and that contributed to the growth of national consciousness. A 'zero sum' model, in which such a consciousness could be developed and sustained only at the expense of other competing consciousnesses, whether local, regional, and international, is inappropriate, however attractive such a 'loyalty-oath' approach to the past might seem.

In practice, there was a diversity and variety of consciousnesses, identities and allegiances. A language of national identity and interest, nation being understood primarily as the subjects of a particular kingdom (rather than of an individual king who might be the ruler of several), was an aspect of awareness and relations at such a level of political, economic, and ecclesiastical activity. That level was of importance in England throughout the Middle Ages, especially because of the territorial continuity of the kingdom, bar on the Scottish frontier, from the tenth century.

In general, activity at the national level did not clash with other aspects of political consciousness, although there were obvious areas of contention, not least over the international dimensions of ecclesiastical activity, and the policies and regional strength of leading magnates. Rather than seeing such contention as the product of rising or falling interests and consciousnesses, it is more appropriate to emphasise the dynamic nature of medieval society, and the degree to which debate and dissension were integral to it, and not inherently alien sources of disruption. As a consequence, the different levels of consciousness were generally symbiotic, and not necessarily a source of conflict.

4

THE NEW NATIONALISM, 1453–1603

This England never did, nor never shall,
Lie at the proud foot of a conqueror,
But when it first did help to wound itself.
Now these her princes are come home again,
Come the three corners of the world in arms,
And we shall shock them. Nought shall make us rue,
If England to itself do rest but true.

In the last speech in *King John* (V, vii), a Shakespeare play probably written in 1596, Philip the Bastard, a fictional illegitimate son of the heroic Richard I (Richard the Lionheart), was clear about national greatness and the consciousness of pride. Nor was this attitude exceptional. In this approach, indeed, Shakespeare captured a wider set of values. For some centuries, church bells were rung every November 17 to celebrate the accession of Elizabeth I in 1558, and thus the end of Catholic rule. Gunpowder Plot bonfires were to follow from 1605. Popular allegiance to Protestantism was an increasingly prominent part of the mix.

The end of the Hundred Years' War in 1453 led to a renewal of an English nationalism, as England became independent of its political links in Europe, as expressed in terms of a territorial commitment. This development represented a culmination of tendencies in the late Middle Ages—the rise of the vernacular, a nationalism expressed in hostility to France, and the development of Parliament.

After the loss of the French territories in 1453, which had a last aftershock in 1558 with the fall of Calais, a possession of the kings of England since 1347, England was insular to a degree that had not been true for centuries. This had consequences for England's diplomatic situation and significance. Under the Treaty of Nonsuch with the Dutch of 1585, England had garrisons in Brill and Flushing, which were 'cautionary towns' held until 1616, as a result of help to the Dutch in their War of Independence with Spain. As the result of another war with Spain, England was also to occupy Dunkirk from its capture from Spain in 1658 until it was sold by Charles II to Louis XIV of France in 1662. With these exceptions, England did not have any Continental possessions from 1558 until the conquest of Gibraltar from Spain in 1704.

More significantly, the concern with Continental possessions and pretensions that had motivated medieval monarchs, and that still played an important role for Henry VIII (r. 1509–47), were of little consequence for Elizabeth I (r. 1558–1603) and for her Stuart successors. Elizabeth sought the return of Calais in 1562, but abandoned the attempt in failure two years later. She again sought its return during her unsuccessful marriage negotiations with the Duke of Anjou, the unimpressive brother of Francis II, Charles IX and Henry III of France, and on other occasions, but the issue was not pressed. Though still claiming to be kings of France (as they did until the reign of George III), the rulers of England were now insular in their possessions and concerns in a fashion that had not been seen since the Norman Conquest of 1066.

And yet, the rulers and political élite of England remained bound closely to Continental affairs, and in some respects more so than in the fifteenth century. Two important aspects of this were the consequences of the Reformation, and the growing strategic significance for England of the Low Countries as a result of the rise of French power and the struggle between the Habsburgs and the Valois rulers of France.

The consequences of the Reformation for religious ties with the Continent were ambiguous. A distinct, and distinctive, independent English Church, free of links with the Papacy, was created. However, in addition, new religious links with Protestant northern Europe, rather than with Rome, led to the establishment of important new ties with that region. Furthermore, English foreign policy now acquired a religious dimension. From the late 1530s, it became apparent that the Reformation would not be universally successful, that, indeed, the Catholic Church and its allies were striking back and with determination, and that this would threaten the English religious settlement and, indeed, due to the question of the legitimacy of Henry VIII's divorce from Catherine of Aragon, the royal succession. As a result, a sense of community of interests with Protestants abroad developed rapidly, initially with the principalities of northern Germany and with Denmark.[1] The early 1560s, moreover, saw the outbreak of confessional violence in France, the Wars of Religion, and this was followed by the Dutch Revolt in which England formally intervened from 1585.

The plight of French Protestants (Huguenots) excited much attention and English troops were sent to France in 1562 and from 1589 to 1597. Elizabeth gave the Huguenot leader, Henry of Navarre (eventually crowned as Henry IV in 1594) considerable support, although her continued backing after his reconversion to Catholicism in 1593 suggests that religion was not the top priority: Elizabeth supported Henry in large part because he was opposed to Spain, with whom he remained at war until 1598.

A key European relationship, both religious and political, was transformed therefore in the sixteenth century by means of the Protestant Reformation. This was to be crucial to English nationalism, as a distinctive religious settlement provided England with particular practices, a unique ecclesiastical history, a specific political narrative, a new role for Crown and Parliament, and a new linkage between centre and localities. In all of these, the break from Rome was the crucial point. Partly as a consequence, the discussion of nationalism from the early sixteenth century does not make much sense in a non-religious context, a point also true for many other states.

Presented as a consequence and source of unity, nationalism, or at least the language of national consciousness, was therefore the product of division and itself divisive. Indeed, it was as national divisions encompassing large numbers outside the élite became politically important that the language of national unity became politically significant. It was part of a process in which élite and non-élite (political) groups were united in a shared identity and common cause, one in which more support could be sought; and also a defence against the disunity of political division.

In the medieval period, there had been serious divisions, but they had generally been largely restricted to the political élite, for example the Wars of the Roses of the second half of the fifteenth century; or had involved popular action against a hostile élite, most obviously the Peasants' Revolt of 1381. The argument cannot be pushed too far, as a language of national interest was employed, most obviously in the reigns of John, Henry III, and Edward II. Nevertheless, the degree of mass-politicisation, the engagement of a large portion of the adult population in politics, was significantly different from that in the Reformation and post-Reformation period. Certainly, a sense of national consciousness existed, and, in Parliament, a mechanism for its expression. Indeed, their interaction helped to lead to the development of each. Parliament, like Continental representative institutions, was very much a medieval creation. It indeed exemplified the process whereby many aspects of the Middle Ages continued across the artificial divide into the 'early-modern period,' indeed developed across this divide. Nevertheless, the combined changes that have been held to usher in this new period altered much. The Reformation and printing were especially important in the process of politicisation and in the changes in the various sorts of collective self-awareness that occurred in the sixteenth century.

Politicisation was not identical with the creation of national consciousness, a point that is highly relevant today. Indeed, politicisation could be at cross-purposes to national consciousness, most obviously through an emphasis on religious heterodoxy and confessional internationalism. A sense of national consciousness did not require mass support, nor indeed an audience. However, literary and other élite definitions of nationhood were of limited resonance unless they could benefit from a degree of politicisation that would widen support, a point that remains relevant.

Politicisation was not a question of a unique turning point, but rather of a continuing situation. Indeed, that was crucial to the definition of a functional nation. Such a process owed much to the Reformation. The confessional struggle existed at every scale and stage from the individual conscience to the eventual apocalyptic outcome and across time, past, present and future, but it was at the national level that the crucial political decisions were made about which faith was to be the established one, and how its worship was to be organised. Similarly, issues of faith and ecclesiastical government, and contemporary hostility to notions of toleration, ensured that these decisions, once made, were to be implemented for the nation and throughout the state. Indeed, distinctive religious arrangements became an expression and definition of state identity, and were opposed to rival interpretations, abroad and at home, and thus to opposing governmental aspirations. The Reformation brought the vernacular Bible and, at Elizabeth I's coronation, the Epistle and the Gospel were read first in Latin and then again in English; the Litany may have been in English. From 1603 on, English was used in place of Latin in the coronation.

The emphasis in England on policy and its defence led to the expression of what was, by the standards of the age, nationalism. This nationalism focused not only on present politics, lay and ecclesiastical, but also on an account of the past; while the politics, in turn, encouraged a fresh interpretation of English history. In the preamble to the Act in Restraint of Appeals [to Rome] of 1533, an Act that proclaimed jurisdictional self-sufficiency and rejected appeals to Rome, it was claimed that 'by divers sundry old authentic histories and chronicles, it is manifestly declared and expressed that this realm of England is an empire, and so hath been accepted in the world, governed by one supreme head and king, having the dignity and royal estate of the imperial crown of the same.' This assertion on behalf of Henry VIII looked back to the House of Wessex's claims of overlordship in Britain in the tenth and eleventh centuries, an overlordship that was rooted in control of England but not restricted to it.

Identity, English nationalism, was enacted every Sunday in churches across the country. It was inculcated in the young with their catechism. It was demonstrated in the placing of the Creed where it could be prominently seen. Indeed, literacy was in part a matter of religious education. Bishops, the key figures in ecclesiastical governance, were appointed and promoted by the Crown.

The historicity and therefore legitimacy of the new Church was a matter for debate between Protestant and Catholic controversialists. Although the British Isles were a setting for confessional rivalry, indeed conflict, the debate in England focused on the particular settlement there. Seeking to minimise the role of the Papacy, Matthew Parker, Archbishop of Canterbury from 1559 to 1575, emphasised the antiquity of the British Church in his *De Antiquitate Britannicae Ecclesiae* (1572). In contrast, Catholics stressed conversion by St Augustine of Canterbury, who had been sent from Rome by Pope Gregory the Great in 597 and who converted the kingdom of Kent, via its ruling house.

The Reformation led not only to fundamental change, doctrinally, liturgically and organisationally, as England separated itself from the universal Church; it also resulted in a religious heterodoxy as many people did not accept the changes, while others sought different changes. This heterodoxy was a challenge to royal authority and power, not least because religious toleration was treated as weakness. At the same time, the idea of transferring the headship of the Church from the Papacy brought a great extension of royal authority and a repositioning of England's role in the world.

Parliament was used under Henry VIII to assert royal control over the Church. The House of Commons was anyway antagonistic to the claims of Church officers. Royal and Parliamentary control were now extended. In 1534, by the Act of Supremacy, Henry became the 'Supreme Head' of the English Church, while the Treason Act of 1534 made it treasonable to deny this supremacy. Conformity in belief, and not just action, was now required. Under this Act, prominent critics, such as Thomas More, the former Chancellor (and later saint), and John Fisher, Bishop of Rochester, were executed in 1535. Henry's policies made the ecclesiastical situation dependent on English politics. Calling the national church, the Church of England was a very clever idea. The Act of Supremacy decreed 'That the King our Sovereign Lord ... shall be taken, accepted and reputed the only Supreme Head on earth of the Church of England called *Anglicana Ecclesia*'. There had been occasional uses of the phrase before 1534, including by the Lollards and John Wycliffe who referred to the Church of England as having a 'stepmother' in Rome.

The destruction of monasteries, nunneries, and shrines overthrew a deeply-grounded set of values and historical accounts. In defence of these values, the rebels in the 1536 Pilgrimage of Grace rallied round the sacred banner of St Cuthbert which was brought by the Durham contingent. The Pilgrims also contrasted 'the whole body of the realm' with 'evil-disposed persons' in the King's Council. This was a contrast with a lengthy medieval pedigree, but one that was made more complex by the religious dimension.

A very different means to present values was offered by the production of an official English Bible in 1537. This was followed by the instruction to every parish church to purchase a copy. As a result of Lollardy, translation of the Bible into English had been associated with heresy, and, in the early sixteenth century, the language was still considered too 'rude' and 'barbarous' for the sacred text. Now, English was to become the language of God's word in Britain, which was an important new dynamic in the culture and politics of its constituent parts. The authoritative nature of the Bible was taken further with the 'Authorized Version', or 'King James Bible' of 1611. Printing was also to reduce the impact of regional linguistic differences. The English religious settlement, which became the Church of England, was distinctive among Protestant churches in government, liturgy and doctrine.

Already fluid, in large part due to Henry VIII's inconstant attitudes, and the murderous political factions at Court, the situation was moved in a markedly Protestant direction under Edward VI (r. 1547–53). Again, Catholic devotional practices and accounts of identity were banned, or at least challenged. Aside from a markedly Protestant Prayer Book, churches were transformed. Their interiors were whitewashed and stripped of imagery, such as statues and wall-paintings. Their removal helped to shatter the pious rituals that gave many people a sense of identity and value.

There was a re-Catholicisation under Mary (r. 1553–8), an episode that, unintentionally and more lastingly, was subsequently very important to the distinctive English national historical tradition; although one that has been lost today. Mary was chiefly remembered as a persecutor, with nearly 300 Protestants publicly burnt at the stake during her reign. One Protestant refugee, John Foxe, published in 1563 his *Acts and Monuments of Matters Most Special and Memorable Happening in the Church*, popularly known as the *Book of Martyrs*. This oft-reprinted account of religious history included a martyrology that was extremely influential in propagating a well-founded image of Catholic cruelty and Protestant bravery that was to sustain a strong anti-Catholic tradition for over 250 years. Foxe presented a history of England as a kingdom that had been in the forefront of the advance towards the Christian faith, and that had not had to be converted by missionaries from Rome. This claim for a separate religious identity encouraged the sense of the English as a chosen people. Such an account might seem a negative, exclusionist definition of nationhood, but the real, as well as apparent, hostile character of international Catholicism helped to justify this position. After an order of 1571, cathedral churches acquired copies of the *Book of Martyrs*, and many parish churches chose to do likewise.

The legacy of Foxe was a long one. Indeed, Foxe was a key writer of, and for, English nationalism, and, in many respects, the key writer. At the time of the Jacobite invasion crisis of late 1745, there were frequent references to the Marian persecutions of 1553–8 and, to that end, a forty-part edition of the *Book of Martyrs* was printed. Foxe's book, moreover, was blended into a more general account of a natural and necessary progress. Thus, in 1759, Richard Rolt, a prolific hack writer, published *The Lives of the Principle Reformers, Both Englishmen and Foreigners, Comprehending the General History of the Reformation; From its beginning in 1360, by Dr John Wickliffe, to its establishment in 1600 under Queen Elizabeth. With an Introduction, wherein the Reformation is amply Vindicated and its necessity fully shown from the Degeneracy of the Clergy, and the Tyranny of the Popes.* Rolt also wrote *A New History of England* (1757), a part-work for children.

The acquisition of copies of the *Book of Martyrs* was one of many steps that became part of a long-term situation and solution thanks to the longevity of the reign of Elizabeth I (r. 1558–1603). Elizabeth produced a Protestant settlement that was moderate by the standards of Edward VI's reign. Crucially, she maintained the authority of bishops. The process by which England avoided a more radical ecclesiastical settlement was also important, and became a significant part of English history. Elizabeth's choice to be termed Supreme Governor of the Church of England, more modest than Supreme Head, may have reflected her position as a woman, but was to be continued by her successors.

Elizabeth protected her settlement and her position against challenges, domestic and foreign. Victory in 1588 over the Spanish Armada, a serious invasion attempt, came to play a critical role in English identity and one that did not diminish with time. Providence was readily seen in a victory that, eventually alongside favourable winds, in practice owed much to a flawed Spanish strategy, the problems of the Spanish navy, luck and the heroism and fighting quality of the English navy. This luck fuelled the development of belief in a Providential sanction to English Protestantism. This sanction was apparently confirmed a century later by the 'Protestant Wind' that helped William of Orange, later William III (r. 1689–1702), to overthrow James II in 1688. That he landed at Torbay on 5 November, Guy Fawkes' Day was another nod to a Providential view of history. What to us illustrates the tenuous survival of Elizabeth's regime, to contemporaries displayed the unassailable nature of divine approval.

The entrenching of the religious settlement through longevity was important to the English experience. The number of people who had experienced a different situation as adults gradually died out, an increasing percentage of the population had been educated in a Protestant Christianity and fewer had lived in an unchallenged world of Catholicism. Moreover Elizabeth was the first ruler not to look into men's consciences: their outward conformity was all she sought. The new religious settlement was associated with an English patriotism, and, indeed, it helped to define it. In the modern secular viewpoint, the impact of the reiterated combination of a particular formulation of Crown and Church is difficult to grasp, but it was successful in ensuring that the Reformation took deep roots.

Protestants did not need to flee abroad, as they had done under Mary. In consequence, confessional links with Continental Protestantism weakened, and Protestantism became less of a Continental import. Conversely, under Elizabeth, many Catholics left for the Continent. The conflation of a sense of national independence with anti-Catholicism and hostility to the leading Continental Catholic powers was greatly encouraged by Elizabeth's reign. As with other episodes in which national consciousness and a rhetoric of national interest were advanced, these actually served a partisan purpose, for national consciousness was defined against domestic as much as foreign opponents, and this definition gave that consciousness a particular political force and urgency. Catholics could be presented, as some prominent ones certainly were, as supporters of hostile foreign powers. These same powers appeared more threatening precisely because of their apparent support within England as well as the British Isles, and uncertainty over the succession made the combination even more threatening.

The result of the Reformation therefore was division and civil strife, a political world of conspiracy, the search for assistance from foreign co-religionists, and regional, social, factional, communal and family differences exacerbated by confessional antagonism. It was a political world in which everything was seen to be at stake because of the prospect and significance of state-directed religious change. In 1570, in the *Bull Regnans in Excelsis*, Pope Pius V condemned Elizabeth as a heretic and released her subjects from their obedience to her. Most English Catholics, however, remained loyal, and this was recognised by the government after the Armada crisis of 1588.

Parliament was an important part of the equation and one that was to be identified with the nation, taking forward the medieval role of Parliament, and also providing a way to place it. Henry VIII's use of Parliament to legitimate his dynastic and constitutional objectives had increased its frequency and role. With the Crown in Parliament as the source of sovereign authority, parliamentary legislation became more common from the 1530s. This was an aspect of the fluidity of the political situation in England, a fluidity that contributed to, and reflected, a particularly dynamic society, one in which social mobility and capitalism affected inherited social roles and positions.[2]

War with Spain from 1585 to 1604 fostered national consciousness and provided a new focus for the commemoration of national history. As popular allegiance to Protestantism grew, so new national days of celebration recalling recent Protestant history became popular. The defeat of the Armada provided an anniversary to match the accession of Elizabeth. Moreover, war with Spain encouraged a new strategic option for England, one in which a global, notably transatlantic, role appeared necessary and inevitable. Religion and war were long presented as playing a positive role in the definition and representation of English nationhood. Thus, in William Stephens' *Thanksgiving Sermon* ...

upon occasion of His Majesty's deliverance from a villainous assassi-nation, preached to the Mayor and Aldermen of London in 1696, when continuity was being sought under William III and during war with France, Elizabeth's policy was presented positively:

> that England should always make itself the head and protection of the whole Protestant interest ... By making all true Protestants, i.e. all true Christians, her friends she enabled England to make good her oldest maxim of state, which is to keep the balance of Europe equal and steady.

At the same time, this approach raises the question of what English nationalism meant to English Catholics. By the late eighteenth century, the tension over Catholic loyalty, which had seen an upsurge from the late 1670s until the 1740s due to James II and the Jacobite movement, was much diminished. Until then, however, this tension had been important to the character of English nationalism.

For the Tudor age, it is also important to consider the develop-ing public culture of the period, as it affected contemporaries and as it influenced succeeding generations. This is notably so with the establishment of a vibrant public theatre and with the appearance of Shakespeare's plays which, alongside the 'King James' or 'Authorised Version' of the Bible (1611), became the canon of Englishness. In addition to the continuation of existing circum-stances and practices, such as the cult of St George, there was a rejection of Latinity, while written English was homogenised with printing and there was much translation into English.

The growth of interest in the antiquarian history of England was also significant. This history was pursued in its own right and as the means to make political points. There was an empha-sis on past glory, as with John Leland's 1544 defence of Geoffrey of Monmouth's account of King Arthur. Anxious to accumulate information on English history, Leland, who was allegedly appointed 'King's Antiquary' in 1533, travelled extensively and wrote much, for example *De Viris Illustribus* (*On Famous Men*).

Shakespeare's plays expressed the aspirations and tensions of the emerging nation state. These could of course be staged in public, while their vocabulary and phrases came to occupy an important position in the language. In *King John*, the Duke of Austria, provides an account of England as a maritime realm:

> ...that England, hedg'd in with the main,
> That water-walled bulwark, still secure
> And confident from foreign purposes. (II, i).

Such an approach employed the resonances of geography in order to underline views on national identity and destiny, and was seen at greater length with John of Gaunt's speech in *Richard II*:

> This royal throne of kings, this sceptr'd isle,
> This earth of majesty, this seat of Mars,
> This other Eden, demi-paradise,
> This fortress built by Nature for herself
> Against infection and the hand of war,
> This happy breed of men, this little world,
> This precious stone set in the silver sea,
> Which serves it in the office of a wall,
> Or as a moat defensive to a house,
> Against the envy of less happier lands,
> This blessed plot, this earth, this realm, this England. (II,i).

This speech was once far more famous than is the case today. It provided many phrases for titles and quotations, particularly for literary works and speeches. In *Edward III* (1592), which is generally credited to Anonymous and Shakespeare, Edward the Black Prince, son of Edward III, brother of John of Gaunt, and father of Richard II, after his sweeping victory over the French at Poitiers in 1356, says to Edward that he wished his hardships were greatly magnified:

so that hereafter ages when they read
The painful traffic of my tender youth
Might thereby be inflamed with such resolve,
As not the territories of France alone,
But likewise Spain, Turkey, and what countries else,
That justly would provoke fair England's ire,
Might at thy presence tremble and retire.[3]

There was a degree of interchangeability, then as later, in nomenclature between England and Britain. Thus, Shakespeare, discussing in his *Henry VIII* (which appeared in 1613, during the reign of James I) the Anglo-French meeting at the Field of the Cloth of Gold (1521) in which Henry VIII and Francis I competed in splendour, has Thomas, 2nd Duke of Norfolk report:

To-day the French,
All clinquant, all in gold, like heathen gods,
Shone down the English; and to-morrow they
Made Britain India: every man that stood
Show'd like a mine... (I, i).

Elizabeth's reported speech in 1588 to the troops assembled at Tilbury east of London to repel the likely Spanish invasion, was for long well-known as an assertion of national pride and resolve, and this has been echoed in recent treatments, notably in the film *Elizabeth: The Golden Age* (2007), which was praised by the Conservative politician Michael Gove:

I can't think of any major motion picture since 1969 (the *Battle of Britain*) in which this country and those who fight on its behalf were paid the compliment of being depicted as good guys, whom history vindicates... What makes it worth celebrating is that it records England historically, as on the side of liberty. Cate Blanchett is magnificent, and her speech when she rallies England's defenders in the cause of freedom against the looming shadow of the Inquisition is a proper and straight interpretation of our past that accurately captures the ideological attachment to liberty which has been the defining factor in our distinctive progress over time.[4]

Darkest Hour (2018), an account of Churchill in 1940, takes this process forward. The 1588 speech displayed some of the rhetorical practices of the period and would have sat well in a Shakespeare play:

> I am come amongst you ... not for my recreation and disport, but being resolved, in the midst and heat of battle, to live and die amongst you all, and lay down for my God and my kingdom and for my people, my honour and my blood, even in the dust. I know I have the body of a weak and feeble woman, but I have the heart and stomach of a king, and of a king of England too, and think foul scorn that [the Duke of] Parma or [the king of] Spain, or any prince of Europe should dare to invade the borders of my realm.

A linkage between religious settlement and cultural progress was frequently asserted, and for long. On 8 November 1729, *The Weekly Journal: or The British Gazetteer* reported the epilogue spoken when the New Theatre was opened in Goodman's Fields, London:

> When Britain first from monkish bondage broke,
> And shook off Rome's imperious, galling yoke,
> When truth and reason were no longer claimed,
> In Popish fetters, and by Priests explained,
> Then wit and learning graced our happy Isle.

In addition, there was an overlap with other processes. Thus, Holinshed's *Chronicles* were among the sources used by Shakespeare, who became a clear and lasting source and symbol of Englishness and who made particular episodes of national history, notably the reigns of Henry IV and Henry V, and the Wars of the Roses, more accessible. The presentation of a distinctive cartographic image was also significant. The mapping of England and, even more, of the parts of England that were pushed through under Elizabeth I, in particular with the extensive work of Christopher Saxton. This mapping further encouraged the sense of national distinctiveness. It was to follow a different course to the more state-controlled map- and chart-making in France.[5]

More generally, the printing of both texts and maps helped, if not to fix language and image, at least to clarify both. This was a contrast to the earlier situation. In the preface to his *Eneydos* (1490), a translation of a French version of the *Aeneid*, William Caxton (c. 1422–c. 1491) recounted a tale of London merchants en route to Zeeland, who stopped in nearby Kent and could not make themselves understood because the Kentish dialect was so strong. One farmer's wife supposedly thought that they were French because their language was so different. Shakespeare frequently plays with dialect as a humorous device, one often linked to travel, distance and the bringing together of strangers, and is able to suggest distance as a result. As the London dialect was based on East Anglian, and was only established in consequence of the massive migration from East Anglia into London during the fourteenth and fifteenth centuries, it was therefore a fairly young standard in the sixteenth century. As Shakespeare would have observed, regional and local differences in spoken English were far stronger than today, both in accent and in words employed. Furthermore, as printing continued much of the medieval dialectalism, the standardization of the printed language emerged slowly, although it was still significant.

More particularly, as with much else, the direction of travel was clear. It was toward a greater degree of national identity and uniformity, one with many variations but, nevertheless, with England and Englishness each more coherent than in the Middle Ages.

5

BRITISH ENGLAND, 1603–1783

In 1603, the end of the main Tudor line, with the long-antici-
pated death of Elizabeth, led to the accession of the Stuarts, the
ruling house of Scotland, in the person of James VI of Scotland
(r. 1567–1603) who became James I of England (r. 1603–25). He
came to the English throne as a result of the marriage in 1503 of
Henry VII's elder daughter, Margaret, with James IV, combined
with the failure of all three of Henry VIII's legitimate children,
only one of whom had married, to have children of their own.
James IV had died fighting the English at the battle of Flodden
(1513), a terrible defeat.

As a result of the personal union of the English and Scottish
thrones, Britishness became a key element in English history in
1603, one that was far more present than it had been earlier in
English history, significant as it had then been. Moreover, this
dimension was more important due to the suppression in the early
1600s of the great rebellion against the Tudor conquest of Ireland.

Thereafter, Englishness was an aspect of a broader pattern of
political identification and contest, such that there was a British
England. Indeed, the number of possible political and religious

outcomes was such that it was a case of British Englands. Pattern might be regarded as an overly bland and optimistic choice of word for a situation that in practice was more variegated, complex, and controversial. Indeed, in part, Englishness came to have a new and uncertain meaning as an aspect of this more complex situation.

James I's accession was managed with far less difficulty than had been anticipated, and, ruling from London, he stayed in England except for one visit back to Scotland. He was therefore less exposed than his Scottish predecessors, notably, but not only, his mother, Mary, Queen of Scots (r. 1542–67), to the impact of quarrels between Scottish lords, or to their defiance of royal authority. She had been deposed and forced to flee to England. Scotland, however, remained an independent state, governed by the Scottish Privy Council and with a separate Parliament. Despite contemporary interest in the example of the recently-devised union of Poland and Lithuania, and James's hopes for a 'union of love,' or, at least, a measure of administrative and economic union, between England and Scotland, the union, in law and fact, remained essentially personal. There was fear in England about the legal and constitutional implications, and the Westminster Parliament rejected a parliamentary or legal bond. Similarly, the union of Portugal and Spain from 1580 to 1640 was solely personal.

From a different direction, Englishness was contested as an element in the breakdown of governance in the British Isles from 1637, a breakdown that eventually led in 1642 to the outbreak of the English Civil War. Englishness had become defined as a public issue and identity that was separate from the state and, more particularly, the Crown. James was criticised for allegedly pro-Spanish policies, an issue that was politically explosive due to the close identification of Spain with Catholicism. The popular rejoicings that followed the failure of the proposed Spanish marriage for the future Charles I, in 1623, indicated the strength of public opinion on a matter that reflected the interrelationships of religion, domestic politics and international relations. The 1624 Parliament provided the basis for war with Spain, helping to channel popular and political enthusiasm for the conflict.

This took forward the situation seen during the medieval Anglo-French monarchy, but gave it a very different iteration. This difference between Crown and Englishness was fostered in large part because of what was presented, under Charles I (r. 1625–49), as a crypto-Catholic assault on the Church of England. With the example of Mary Tudor (r. 1553–8) already present, at least to Protestants, Charles helped to provide an idea of the nation that to some excluded the monarchy, indeed an idea that focused on religion, the most significant feature in identity and politics, whether national or local.

At the same time, the political crisis began not in England but in Scotland, and because of strong opposition there to Charles's ham-fisted ecclesiastical policies. Thus, there was a British, as well as international, dimension to the religious opposition to Charles, one in which the Arminianism of Archbishop Laud in England, the stress on episcopacy in Scotland, the apparent support for Catholics in Ireland, the crypto-Catholicism of Court society in Whitehall Palace, and the diplomatic alignment with Spain in the 1630s, could all be related to the marked advance of Catholicism on the Continent in the early stages of the Thirty Years' War (1618–48).

In England, tension in the 1620s led to a revival of ringing bells for the accession day of Elizabeth I, recalling times past when the monarch had been clearly identified with the successful pursuit of what were generally seen as national interests. Forgetting the serious problems of the time, Elizabeth's war with Spain was recalled as triumphant as well as being truly national in being anti-Catholic and naval. The recent past was deployed as a history lesson in appropriate nationalism, a practice also seen at present. However, the wars begun with both France and Spain in the 1620s proved not only short but also unsuccessful.

The Civil Wars (1642–6, 1648) and the subsequent Interregnum (1649–60) led to a series of 'British' solutions; solutions, however, that, in many respects, represented a greater Englishness. The Parliamentary regime in England relied heavily on Scottish intervention (intervention by the Scottish opponents of the Crown) in England in 1644–6, notably in the battle of Marston Moor in 1644, a battle that settled the fate of the North. Nevertheless, the victorious side in England then fell out with the Scots. This was largely over the treatment of Charles I, but also over the religious settlement, with the Scots insisting on a Presbyterian outcome in accordance with the situation within Scotland. In England, in contrast, the army preferred an Independent outcome, which would permit independent congregations that were not under Presbyterian control.

Both options reflected the extent to which an episcopalian Church of England was not an inevitable aspect of English identity and thus nationalism. Instead, political contingencies came to play a key role. This is not the same as the latter idea of nations as invented communities, for there was a nation the character and future of which were contested. Moreover, options were also set by the past. There was no chance in the 1640s that English nationalism would be defined as Catholic.

Negotiations between the Scots and the Royalists led, in 1648, to a turnabout in which they allied in an attempt to overthrow the government in England, only for both to be rapidly routed in what was to be known as the Second Civil War. Indeed, the overwhelming defeat of the Scottish invading army by Oliver Cromwell at Preston in 1648 was one of the most important battles in both British and English history.

War radicalised the revolution. In the aftermath, a republic was declared, Charles was tried and executed (1649), and the

Parliamentary army successfully conquered Scotland, Ireland, and the surviving Royalist outliers, from the Scilly Isles to the colonies in North America.

With the exception of Edward I's brief succession in subjugating Scotland, this represented the first time in which the entire British world had been conquered. It was followed by a series of political experiments. In these, Cromwell, the leading Parliamentary general, played a central role as he sought a settlement that was at once stable and righteous. The constitutional rejigging included in 1653, with Barebone's Parliament (named after a radical member, Praise-God Barebone), a British Parliament, the first of its type. However, in reality, the representation from Scotland and Ireland was largely a matter of English army officers. The failure of this Parliament led Cromwell, later that year, to become Lord Protector 'of England, Scotland, Ireland etc'. On 22 January 1655, when addressing Parliament, he referred to 'the people of these nations.' At the same time, Cromwell was very much associated with England, indeed was 'God's Englishman'.[1]

Cromwell was certainly willing to provide a new political geography. Thus, in 1655, largely in response to unsuccessful Royalist risings, authority in the localities was entrusted to major-generals, instructed to preserve security and create a godly and efficient kingdom. The division of the country among the eleven major-generals created a new geography. It was a geography of military control that totally ignored long-established patterns based on aristocratic estates and clientages. The major-generals might have a role akin to that of Tudor lords lieutenant, but their social background and political goals were very different.

Much of the political history of 1637–1707 was an attempt to work out a political solution to the diversity of the British Isles. At that level, there was not the compactness or ability readily to reach a solution that was generally shown in England, an ability that owed much to the development and operation there of parliamentary monarchy. The role of Parliament in articulating and encapsulating a sense of national identity and interest cannot be removed from the partisan context in which that was contested, but that very context helped to accentuate this role, especially in the seventeenth century.

Charles II benefited from the willingness in Britain to see the restoration of Stuart monarchy in 1660, as well as from the specific politics of that year. In the Restoration, the old, pre-Civil War, constitutional separations within the British Isles prevailed: there was to be no British Parliament under the restored Stuarts. Subsequently, in Church and state, the contested nature of Englishness and its relationship with meanings and ideas of Britishness, then played out through the exclusion of James II in the Glorious Revolution (1688), the Revolution Settlement (1689), the Act of Settlement (1701), the parliamentary union with Scotland (1707), the impacts on identity of the Hanoverian succession (1714), the crises of Jacobite rebellions (1715–16 and 1745–6), and notably the Jacobite invasion of England (1745), and the eventual overthrow of the link with the North American colonies (1775–83).

The list of conflicts appeared appropriate, for struggle, including wars with foreign powers, was a central theme in national identity. This theme was enacted in Handel's oratorios as he compared England with Old Testament Israel. Indeed, nationalism was the product of struggle. Nationalism also offered the history and record of struggle, as well as its defence. Accounts of this struggle in foreign seas and lands resonated for those at home.

This struggle had a moral character that is difficult to capture today. There was struggle against vice, international and domestic, political and religious, a theme that linked moralists who had very different political prospectuses, but that also captured the moral obligations of statehood. This is an aspect of nationalism that is less clear today. Liberty and religion seemed to be dependent upon the moral calibre of the people, and this calibre was threatened by subversion encouraged by poor governance. Each achievement was no more than a stage upon the road, as nationhood had to be defended, and not least if the country wished to be ensured the support of Providence. This defensiveness accorded with the belief that Anglo-Saxon liberties had been overthrown by the Norman Conquest.

Queen Mary II, William III's wife and co-ruler in 1689–94, and her sister, Queen Anne (r. 1702–14), neither of whom visited Ireland, Scotland or Wales, both emphasised their Englishness. The prime questions here are what was the impact of England on the variety of Britains on offer, and, in contrast, of the impact of this variety on England. Moreover, there was the issue of what England and Englishness meant in this period. Given the action-reaction model of identity and action, there is, in particular, the issue of how far attitudes to Englishness arose in reaction to aspects of Britishness and, more especially, the perception of them. This was in part addressed in the eighteenth century by the formulation of a Britishness that, to the English, was essentially coterminous with Englishness.

Indeed, repeatedly, this formulation helps answer the question of what happened to the overlapping facets of English identity, Englishness, and English nationalism, during the period of 'British ascendancy' from 1707. They did not go underground but, instead, essentially defined Britishness for the English. This co-identification helped them to present those inhabitants of the British Isles who did not fit in with these norms as in some respects unBritish because they were unEnglish. Indeed, this is a reminder of the fundamentally political character of nationalism, in so far as politics rests on the anthropology and psychology of group dynamics.

The Union of 1707, creating the kingdom of Great Britain, arose essentially from English concern about the possible hazards posed by an autonomous or independent Scotland as a result of a different succession to the childless Anne, and from Scottish economic weakness: the Scots did not wish to be shut out from the English and colonial market. The Union gave Scotland 45 MPs in the Westminster House of Commons and 16 peers, elected by an assembly of Scottish peers, in the House of Lords. This was an under-representation of Scotland's population, but an over-representation of its economic strength. The terms were negotiated in 1706 and ratified by the Scottish Parliament on 16 January 1707. In 1708, the new Parliament of Great Britain abolished the Scottish Privy Council, the principal executive agency for Scotland, and thus ensured that there would be one British Privy Council sitting in London.

The total defeat of the Jacobites in 1746, and the subsequent remodelling of the governance of the Scottish Highlands, with the abolition of hereditable jurisdictions, aided this process as the loyalist Scots were regarded in England as part of the process of orderly progress that the Hanoverian Whig Ascendancy presented itself as in succession to those who had supported the Glorious Revolution and the Revolution Settlement. The crushing of the '45, more directly, ensured that the new British state created by the parliamentary union of 1707 would continue to be one whose political tone and agenda were set in London and southern England. This was the basis of British consciousness, a development that did not so much alter the views of the English political élite, for whom Britain was essentially an extension of England, but, rather, that reflected the determination of the Scottish, and, to a lesser extent, Welsh and Irish Protestant elites to link their fate with that of the British state; indeed the Anglican élite in Ireland persisted in defining itself as English.

British history seen as starting in 1707 and cemented in 1745–6 is an approach that focuses not only on union with Scotland, but also on the Revolution Settlement. The ideas of limited government, representative politics, accountable monarchy, the rule of law, and a degree of religious freedom, were all affirmed from 1689. Partly as a result, these ideas have all been part of Britain's deep history. Indeed, their roots were longer-lasting. By the Bill of Rights of 12 February 1689, Parliament misleadingly declared that James II had deserted England. This was a product of the preference for the view that James had abdicated, rather than the more radical notion that he had been deposed. Part of the character inscribed on the nation from then was that of moderation, although that was a highly subjective presentation. Declaring, 'whereas it hath been found by experience that it is inconsistent with the safety and welfare of this Protestant kingdom to be governed by a popish prince, or by any king or queen marrying a papist,' Parliament also debarred all Catholics from the succession, a measure only repealed in 2013.

The financial settlement left William with an English ordinary revenue that was too small for his peacetime needs, obliging him to turn to Parliament for support. This was a result of the distrust of the royal prerogative that had arisen as a result of Stuart rule. So also was the clause in the Bill of Rights prohibiting a standing army unless with the agreement of Parliament. Again, aspects of what would later be seen as Englishness in part arose from contingent political circumstances.

Such a development of Britishness did not, however, prevent the coincident yet still vigorous senses of local, provincial, and national identities. The distinctive English Common Law tradition was significant as a cause of legal, intellectual and political divergence from the Continent. Although it is also possible to emphasise the continuity of Natural Law traditions in England, the Common Law was very different from the Continental Roman Law. More recently, the relative political and judicial decline, notably in the face of international jurisdictions, of the Common Law has helped to lessen English exceptionalism.

In Scotland, Episcopacy had been abolished as the state religion in 1689 and a Presbyterian Church established the following year. This arrangement was not overthrown and, as a result, the Union of 1707 led to the creation of a multi-confessional state. In part, this situation repeated the earlier combination of Englishness with the linguistic, cultural, and ethnic diversity of an England that stretched from Cornwall, whose distinctive language only reportedly disappeared with Dorothy (Dolly) Pentreath (c. 1692–1777), to the Scottish borders. In 1776, an American traveller recorded of Shropshire: 'Call the people in this country Welsh and you offend them: go into Wales and you can offer them no greater insult than to call them English. Is this Patriotism? It is a love of one's own country.'[2] And yet, the sense of separate identity was weakened, especially at the level of the élite, by the decline of Celtic languages and the growing appeal of English cultural norms and customs, including linguistic standardisation.[3]

In the early eighteenth century, there was some support for union with England among Irish Protestants, but it was unsuccessful. Legislation in Westminster, the result of protectionist lobbying by English interests, hindered Irish exports, especially to English and colonial markets. In addition, the granting of Irish lands and pensions to favoured English courtiers exacerbated the problem of absentee landowners and revenue-holders, with a consequent drain on money out of Ireland, much to the anger of Jonathan Swift.

Ireland retained its Parliament until the Act of Union of 1800 and the need to manage this Parliament obliged London-based politicians to turn to Irish 'undertakers.' This was not an easy process, as they could never be certain who in Ireland could be trusted with political power or for how long. The preservation of a Dublin Parliament enabled Ireland's Protestant politicians to retain a measure of importance and independence, so that

London faced difficulties in devising effective strategies for governing Ireland.

Crucial to the creation of the Whig Ascendancy in England was what was termed the Whig approach, which emphasised a Protestant identity for the nation, respect for property, the rule of law, and parliamentary sovereignty as a means to secure liberty. This approach combined a patriotic sense of national uniqueness with a frequently xenophobic contempt for foreigners. History was presented as moving in an inevitable direction, and that as being one of steady improvement, which offered a teleological progressivism. English national consciousness, and thus patriotism, were given a tremendous boost and fresh definition by the Glorious Revolution, but this consciousness was politically defined and partisan. It was directed against Jacobites and those held likely to support the exiled Stuarts, especially Catholics in England and, although to a lesser extent, Episcopalians in Scotland. It was also directed against Louis XIV of France (r. 1643–1715), the cousin and ally of Charles II and the cousin and principal patron of the exiled James II (and VII of Scotland). Louis established himself as the national enemy from 1689, and more by his real and apparent backing for the Stuarts and their British supporters, than by his aggressive activities on the Continent against Britain's allies. Indeed, in previous conflicts, Charles II had not fought Louis, but instead allied with him against the Dutch in 1672–4 in the Third Anglo-Dutch War. However, the brutal treatment of the Huguenots (French Protestants) in the 1680s was also important in affecting British attitudes.

Due to the overthrow of James II (and VII), English, still more British, patriotism was, after 1688, necessarily divisive, and derived much of its drive from its partisan character. The Glorious Revolution led to the development of two competing theses of patriotism, one of which triumphed, and was able therefore to define patriotism accordingly. Such a process was not new. Indeed, it was a key aspect of the lengthy Reformation crisis. A national culture was defined accordingly. Handel's oratorios joined the authority of the Biblical story to rallying patriotic enthusiasm.[4]

In the dedication of 1760 to the fourteenth edition of his *A New History of England*, the prolific writer John Lockman 'endeavoured to set the whole in such a light as may inspire the readers with an ardent love for our pure religion, and its darling attendant, liberty; and, on the other hand, with a just abhorrence of popery, and its companion, slavery.' By slavery, English and British commentators referred to the situation in Britain, and not that across the empire from which they benefited, in short to political control and not the use of labour for economic purposes. This was Englishness defined by means of being different from Frenchness. So also as different to a feudal past that had seemed all-too-present in the shape of support for Jacobitism among Highland Scots and among Englishmen living in marginal political communities: marginal because reactionary and reactionary because marginal.

Thus, Lockman's remarks captured the clear ideological framing of a sense of distinctive nationhood. This framing took place in large part in opposition to apparent threats, which reflected the extent to which responses to challenges were significant to national identity and to government policy, notably foreign and military. This proved an effective mechanism for unity and identity, unity in identity and identity in unity, until recent decades when it appears to have broken down.

This Whiggish account did not satisfy all, and there was a vibrant Tory critique that sought to focus on a more defined Englishness. This critique was one in which the preservation of the Church of England played a greater role. Moreover, the Englishness offered by the Tories was anti-cosmopolitan, if not xenophobic. This was clearly displayed in 1753 by the crisis over

Jewish naturalisation. An Act to that end was reversed due to public agitation.[5]

There was also hostility to Protestant immigrants, especially Huguenots from France and 'poor Palatines' from Germany. In part, this hostility was religious in character, as, although Latitudinarians within the Church of England were sympathetic to Continental Protestants, the position of the Church appeared to Tories to be under threat from Whig attitudes and policies. A dilution of the Englishness of the Church of England was an important aspect of this apparent threat. The Huguenots and the Palatines were presented as allies of the Whigs.

Nationalism was cumulative, a matter of past as well as present, structures as well as events, but was also open to a variety of interpretations. That variety was particularly to the fore during crises. Thus, the American War of Independence saw very different accounts of English nationalism advanced. This was clear when John Adams, America's first ambassador to Britain, toured England in 1786 with Thomas Jefferson, who was visiting from his ambassadorial post in Paris. In his diary, Adams recorded:

> Edgehill and Worcester were curious and interesting to us, as scenes where freemen had fought for their rights. The people in the neighbourhood appeared so ignorant and careless at Worcester, that I was provoked, and asked, 'And do Englishmen so soon forget the ground where liberty was fought for? Tell your neighbours and your children that this is holy ground; much holier than that on which your churches stand. All England should come in pilgrimage to this hill once a year'.

To Adams, what he saw was clear. A people ignorant of their past and with a lost nationalism, one, indeed, that might be a precursor of the modern situation. Edgehill (1642) was the first battle of the English Civil War and Worcester (1651), Oliver Cromwell's last victory, brought to a decisive end the Stuart attempt to defeat the Parliamentarian regime. However, it is worth, as so often when citing or contextualising evidence, to extend quotations and expand consideration. Adams continued: 'This animated them, and they seemed much pleased with it. Perhaps their awkwardness before might arise from their uncertainty of our sentiments concerning the civil wars.'[6] Conversely, in Worcester, there was a more Royalist culture, as revealed by the contents of Valentine Green's *History and Antiquities of the City and Suburbs of Worcester* (1764) and the highly positive response to George III's visit in 1788, and those who held these views would not have sympathised with Adams. The Parliamentarian troops had inflicted serious damage in Worcester in 1651.

The sense and stability of the locality was a building block to that of the nation, and if the opposite was also true, it was less the case. For example, the *Notitia Monastica, or a Short History of the Religious Houses in England and Wales* (1695) by Thomas Tanner, Bishop of St Asaph, was in effect a national collection of local history. The relationship between locality and nation, culturally and politically, remains significant, but does not attract sufficient attention.

The role of religion was crucial because it differentiated England (and Wales) from Scotland and Ireland. Much of the politics of the seventeenth century was a matter of the 'processing' of the union of the crowns in 1603, and this process continued until the crushing defeat of Jacobitism at the battle of Culloden in 1746. The key decision on the political level might be that of a loss of separate identity as a result of the union of the London and Edinburgh parliaments in 1707 and, with that, the clearer creation of a British political identity. Yet, from the religious perspective, this was far less the case. England and Scotland were anti-Catholic, and that provided a clear cement of Britishness. Yet, they also had rival Protestant establishments, and the contrast between the Church of England and the Church of Scotland was highly significant to the continued separateness of the two. That the Church of Scotland, with its Calvinism and its organisation, was also closer to English Protestant alternatives (and Continental Protestant ones) than to the Church of England highlighted the contrast and increased tension.

Had there been a union of England and Scotland at the religious level, in the sense of a common Church structure, liturgy and much else, then this would have encouraged a joining of national histories. Instead, the Scots in part defined themselves by successfully pursuing and defending a distinctive religious settlement. In turn, this encouraged a sense of separation in, and from, England. As a result, much that focused on the Church was in effect a pursuit of nationalism. Religious works could sell extremely well. *The Church Catechism Explained by Way of Question and Answer, and Confirm'd by Scripture Proofs* (1700) by the Kent cleric John Lewis, a keen defender of the Church of England, went through forty-two editions by 1812. It was not alone: 10,000 copies of Robert Nelson's *A Companion for Festivals and Fasts of the Church of England* (1704) were printed in four and a half years, and a 30th edition appeared in 1826. Anti-Catholicism was a key part of the equation. *The Preservative Against Popery* tracts of the 1680s were enormously popular and influential in the eighteenth century.

Given that most of the English viewed events in their own age as directly driven by God, including the Jacobite defeats of 1715 and 1745, the growth of empire, military victories, and even the London earthquakes of 1692 and 1750, it was not surprising that nationhood was held to reflect the intervention and support of Providence. The idea of Britain (in practice England) as an 'elect nation' and a second Israel, chosen by God, contributed to contemporary exceptionalism and also to a sense of historical distinctiveness. Handel's *Samson* (1743) was performed eight times in its first season, a considerable triumph, while the celebrations of his work which were held in 1784–91 and supported by George III, showed the continuing popularity of his approach.

In these and other works, elect status was seen to develop from a long sequence of events that justified God's endorsement. This approach could be traced back not only to the Reformation, but further into a distant past that included Edward the Confessor (r. 1042–66), who was first claimed to have the power to cure the 'King's Evil' (a practice only discontinued in 1714), and even to more mythological, but powerful, figures like king Arthur, as well as to king Alfred, a real figure. The medievalism that became increasingly significant in the second half of the century, but could already be seen in the 1730s, made much of this English 'deep history,' and, notably, of Alfred. Anglo-Saxonism took on a new energy.

Moreover, the ambient identification of nationalism with divine support meant that the recording of Providential sanction was of great significance for the idea of nationhood. Religious perspectives remained important to this idea into the late twentieth century, and current concerns about Islamic identity and supranational loyalty reflect their continued salience.

The significance of religion also rested on its ability to be socially inclusive, unlike the culture of print which essentially excluded the illiterate. As such, religion interacted with a folk culture in which the past was very much a living presence. This was a process brilliantly satirised by Laurence Sterne in his novel *Tristram Shandy* (1759–67).

Historical works readily found Providence the key defender of nationhood, and history-writing thus an appropriate way to assert nationalism. In his dedication of volume two of his history of England to George I, Laurence Echard, a clergyman, presented the Glorious Revolution as 'wonderful and providential'. He also wrote:

> England in an especial manner has been such a mighty and distinct scene of action, in the latter ages of the world, that during the compass of this History, there appears a greater variety of changes, gov-

ernments and establishments; and there seems to have been more visible and signal instances of judgements and punishments, mercies and deliverances from above, then perhaps can be paralleled in any other part of the Western world.

The text of this book was very clear that 'Divine Providence' played a key role, not least due to the lapsed nature of mankind as a consequence of Adam's Fall.[7] This lapsed nature made divine support even more necessary, a point valid for nations as well as individuals, this-time as well as all-time. The Restoration of Stuart monarchy in 1660 was described accordingly as 'the most free and exalted expression of a delivered and overjoyed nation, triumphantly restored, without one drop of blood, by the All-merciful and powerful Hand of Heaven.'[8] National history and identity, the two mutually dependent, could not be separated from Providence. The perfectability of society was not at the behest of humans, and the emphasis on Providence as understood in the period inherently cut across any idea of a solution for Humanity as a whole.

Echard was a moderate Tory, and the Whigs added a powerful theme of human intervention in the shape of the balance of power. This interpretation permitted a representation of England in terms of moderation, which was to be a standard theme in the self-presentation of English distinctiveness. Indeed, a key source was that of the supposed middle way or *via media* in Church matters between radical Protestantism and Catholicism. This account drew on Classical ideas of moderation. In political terms, there was a standard Aristotelian tension between royal prerogatives and popular privileges, a tension that, at its best, produced a balance that guaranteed liberty. The Saxon *witan* and the post-1688 Parliament were presented as the prime instances of this balance, and there was a ready reading, and forward and back, from one to the other.

The dedication in 1744 to Frederick, Prince of Wales, by Nicholas Tindal, an Anglican clergyman, of a translation of Paul de Rapin-Thoyras's influential Whiggish history of England, set out this theme:

> you will see here the origin and nature of our excellent constitution, where the prerogatives of the Crown, and Privileges of the subject are so heavily proportioned, that the King and the People are inseparably united in the same interests and views. You will observe that this union, though talked of by even the most arbitrary princes with respect to their subjects, is peculiar to the English monarchy, and the most solid foundation of the sovereign's glory, and the people's happiness.
>
> Accordingly, you will constantly find, that in the reigns where this union was cultivated, the kingdom flourished, and the prince was glorious, powerful, trusted, beloved. On the contrary, when, by an arbitrary disposition, of evil counsels, it was interrupted, the constitution languished, mutual confidence vanished, distrust, jealousy, discord arose; and when entirely broken ... confusion and civil wars ensued.

Similar views were found in the writings of George Lyttelton, who was a Whig MP as well as an author, including of history. He saw a longstanding English identity which he traced back to the Saxon system of limited royal power. This was then presented as surviving the Norman Conquest, only for a division to open up between the 'nobles' and 'the people,' with the former a burden on the latter. Lyttelton praised the reign of Elizabeth as coming 'to an equal balance, which is the true perfection of it,' only to degenerate under the Stuarts, before revival as a result of the Glorious Revolution: 'the government was settled on a new foundation, agreeable to the ancient Saxon principles from which it had declined'.[9]

This understanding of a revolution as a return to past circumstances, and, ideally, to a past golden age that had been lost as a consequence of usurpations of some type, was a significant variant on the progressivism or improvability with which Whig thought is associated. The account of 1688–9 as a Glorious Revolution made it possible to reconcile both views and sets of images, and this helped Whiggism to act as a potent and reso nant ideology. Moreover, the continuing importance of the Revolution Settlement as a later version of Magna Carta was readily apparent. Multiple themes, interpretations, and echoes, like identities, are significant, and were located in terms of a lasting struggle.

Yet, the construction of nationalism in these historical national terms was in part challenged by the accession of the Dutch William of Orange as William III (r. 1689–1702), and then by the accession of the Elector of Hanover as George I (r. 1714–27), which began a dynastic link with Hanover that lasted until 1837. The foreignness of the monarch helped to accentuate the role of Parliament. Such foreignness was not so much a mat- ter of the Scottish, Dutch or Hanoverian origin of the monarchs after 1603, although that could be important, and could lead to the idea of a foreign takeover, but, rather, of their real, or appar- ent, religious and ecclesiastical views. This was an aspect of the role of religion in national identity. That William III, George I, and George II (r. 1727–60), were clearly identified with the Whigs helped to make their origins and interests vulnerable to attack by the Tories, and further complicated understandings of nationalism. At the same time, each was a Protestant and willing to support the position of the Church of England, albeit not as much as many of its supporters sought.

In hindsight, the parliamentary link with Scotland appeared the key one, but in political terms that with Hanover was more important during the reigns of George I and George II. That is an aspect of the politics of the period that has been lost to public attention, but one that has interesting resonances in current con- troversies over Britain's European links. At the same time, there are no direct parallels.

Politics played a crucial role in the deployment and development of history. Historians engaged actively in the controversies of the period. Thus, in 1747, appeared the first volume of *A General History of England*. Dedicated to the Duke of Beaufort, a prominent Tory with Jacobite leanings, it was written by Thomas Carte, a Jacobite and Nonjuror (High Church Anglicans who refused to accept William III as king due to their oaths of allegiance to James II), who described himself as 'an Englishman' and, thus, by extension not pro-Hanoverian. The fourth volume presented the execution of Charles I in 1649 in strongly religious terms: 'died a martyr for the liberties of his people, and the rights of the Church of England'. This approach offered an anti-, or at least, non-, Whig account of national history and thus nationalism. Indeed, Carte's work reflected lasting themes in Toryism.

However, nationalism was to be redefined as a result of the integration of Toryism into a national political culture and language in mid-century. This integration reflected sweeping victory over France and Spain in the Seven Years' War (1756–63), and the accession, with George III (r. 1760–1820), of a king who had conspicuously broken with the Hanoverian identity of his two predecessors, George I and George II. George III continued to care about Hanover and to try to advance its interests, but he never visited it.

The 1760s also saw a strong focus on national cultural interests, notably with the foundation of the Royal Academy in 1768 and the Shakespeare Jubilee in 1769. The Academy was the realisation of long-held ideas for an institution that would combine artistic education with national glory. In 1772, Joshua Reynolds, the President of the Academy, could depict England as more dynamic than France. Samuel Johnson attempted to fix the English language with his massive *Dictionary*. The well-read Elizabeth Montagu observed to a friend in 1762: 'Few people know anything of the English history but what they learn from

Shakespeare; for our story is rather a tissue of personal adventures and catastrophes than a series of political events.' In combination, these cultural elements reflected a powerful endorsement of a sense of distinctiveness, one, in particular, that was defined in terms of ideas of Englishness. William Blackstone, appointed in 1758, the first Vinerian Professor of English Law at Oxford, published the *Commentaries on the Laws of England* (1765–9), in part to acclaim Common Law against Roman Law.

There was no comparable Britishness involved, although in part a lack of precision in England provided such a Britishness. For example, 'An old-fashioned Englishman,' in a letter printed in the *St James's Chronicle* of 13 May 1769, claimed:

> We are a people that should be often roused to a sense of our blessings, and to the means of securing them. French clothes, French cookery, French literature, French plays, French shoes, and French hats, have so possessed us from top to toe, that if we do not guard against these encroaching refinements, we shall have even our immortal Shakespeare plucked from his eminence by French critics, and degraded to the character of buffoon and drunken savage, which the spirit of envy and ignorance has been pleased to call him by the pen of Monsieur de Voltaire ... while we can think and feel like Britons, we shall ever glory in the immortal productions of the greatest poet which any age or country has produced.

Culture was essentially defined against France and Italy, the former notably in art and the latter in music, although other elements played a role. There had long been pressure for changing the language of the law from (old) French and Latin to English, and this was achieved in 1731. There was an emphasis on the supposed truthfulness of English culture and on the alleged artfulness and artificiality of its opponent. Culture was presented in terms of rivalry. Key issues included the language used in opera, specifically the preference for English, as in John Gay's *The Beggar's Opera* (1728), rather than Italian, the patronage of foreign as opposed to native performers, resistance to the presence of Catholic images, and the engagement with the past.[10] Popular images and stereotypes included John Bull.

In the eighteenth century, the public market for an explicitly English engagement with English culture and history became far stronger, in turn creating models for the future. Even if a shared inheritance, the past was interpreted to emphasise Englishness. This was seen with the shared Classical heritage which could reflect differences in literary and political culture as contrasts in that heritage were highlighted. Thus, in England, the French were seen as fawning followers of Horace, civilised, urbane, sophisticated, fashionable servants or slaves, but the English as rugged, no-nonsense, plain-speaking, followers of Juvenal, and hence free. The glory of Augustan Rome encompassed both Horace and Juvenal, but in England there was an important theme of Classical republican virtue that looked back to Rome before the emperors, as in Joseph Addison's popular play *Cato* (1713).

Moreover, the model of a progressive society, although it owed much to the Scottish Enlightenment, was perceived abroad as English. For example, French and German historians and lawyers talked about England, not Britain. Foreign travellers focused on England, and, indeed, as with Montesquieu and Voltaire, London. An English political culture had not only survived union with Scotland in 1707; it had been strengthened by it.

Moreover, England was working more effectively as a national unit, in part because of a great change in transport routes, the most important since the Romans built their roads. By 1750, a sizeable network of new turnpikes radiating from London had been created. London and north-west England were well linked, with the road to Chester and both roads to Manchester turnpiked for most of their length. The time of journeys fell, while their frequency rose. The time of a journey from Manchester to London fell from three days in 1760 to 28 hours in 1788, while average speeds between London and Birmingham rose to fifteen miles an hour. The first regular Norwich-London coach service taking less than a day started in 1761, and by 1783 there were 25 departures a week from Norwich to London, as well as two departures of stage wagons carrying goods. On 19 June 1773, *Jackson's Oxford Journal* reported:

> The difference in the number of stage coaches, etc. travelling on the Western road, within these few years, is not a little remarkable. About ten years ago there only passed through Salisbury in the course of a week, to and from London and Exeter, six stage coaches, which carried six passengers each, making in the whole (if full) 36 passengers. At present there constantly pass, between the above places, in the same space of time, 24 stage coaches, carrying six passengers each, and 28 stage chaises, carrying three each, making in the whole, if full, 228 passengers.

There was no comparable linkage with Scotland and Ireland. At any rate, business and fashion focused on London. The nation was being closely integrated, a process that had cultural consequences, as in the improved circulation and distribution of newspapers and letters, and, with them, news and opinion. A joined-up nation became more apparent.

6

ENGLISHNESS AND EMPIRE, 1783–1967

ALL.
He is an Englishman!
BOAT.
He is an Englishman!
For he himself has said it,
And it's greatly to his credit,
That he is an Englishman!
ALL.
That he is an Englishman!
BOAT.
For he might have been a Roosian,
A French, or Turk, or Proosian,
Or perhaps Itali-an!
ALL.
Or perhaps Itali-an!
BOAT.
But in spite of all temptations
To belong to other nations,
He remains an Englishman!
He remains an Englishman!

ENGLISH NATIONALISM

ALL.

For in spite of all temptations
To belong to other nations,
He remains an Englishman!
He remains an Englishman!

Gilbert and Sullivan, *HMS Pinafore*, 1878.

The relationship between English identity and nationalism on one hand, and Britain as the great empire and the leading economic power on the other, was a complex one, and this complexity affects the discussion of the recent century. For long, there was a cultural Britishness and a lack of Scottish and Welsh separatism. Ireland, however, was very different and far more open to distinctive narratives. If, in part, the British Empire and Britishness were expressions of Englishness, this was not the Englishness of current days.

Empire, in the nineteenth century and for part of the twentieth, was a major part of a narrative of success and an exceptionalism that were closely related to economic strength. In turn, this strength was part of a narrative of success and an account of exceptionalism closely related to Empire. The notions of progress inherent to the Whig approach were, as with 'the first industrial nation,' readily applied to define modernity. In this account, Englishness was intrinsically linked to a big bang of modernity, in which the Industrial Revolution played a crucial role, indeed was a definition of modernity. That Scotland was a key player did not detract from this view of Englishness. Developments in England, including industrialisation, urbanisation, and imperialism, were aspects of a wider Western process. That was not, however, the general perception *in* England, which flourished on notions of exceptionalism. Moreover, common trends do not in themselves undermine distinctiveness.

There was a sense, instead, of the country as distinctive and foremost, and the latter a reflection of this distinctiveness while also helping to constitute it; this sense has to be taken into account in assessing its history. The lack of any serious break-down in social and political stability were important to the discussion of exceptionalism. In contrast to many Continental states, there was no political revolution in England, either at the time of the French Revolutionary crisis at the close of the eighteenth century, or in the mid-nineteenth century, when there were revolutions across the Continent. The agitation surrounding the First Reform Act in 1832 or Chartism in 1848 was a pale shadow of disorder in France, Spain, Portugal, or the German and Italian states. As a result, there was no political punctuation point at which a written constitution was established that might have more precisely defined the nation.

Indeed, during the French Revolutionary and Napoleonic Wars (1793–1815), radicalism was discredited as allegedly pro-French. In contrast, Throne and Altar ideology became stronger in reaction to the ideas associated with the French Revolution and its English supporters. Toryism was re-created as a politics of patriotism and nationalism. That owed much to the ideological and political pressures, issues and contingencies of that decade. At the same time, Toryism as the politics of patriotism and nationalism also echoed more traditional themes. In turn, patriotism and nationalism greatly informed nineteenth-century attitudes. Aside from their role in Toryism, they were also significant for liberalism, albeit without the crucial component of the traditional political support for the Church of England.

Edmund Burke (1730–97), an Irishman who sat in the Westminster Parliament from 1766 to 1794, was important to the definition of Englishness for a new century. He argued, in his deliberately provocative, and immediately controversial (and by many celebrated) *Reflections on the Revolution in France* (1790), that developments in France were harmful because they were unrelated to any sense of continuity, indeed any historical consciousness. In contrast, at the Restoration of the Stuart dynasty in 1660, and with the Glorious Revolution overthrowing the authoritarian James II in 1688–9, the English, according to Burke:

> regenerated the deficient part of the old constitution through the parts which were not impaired. They kept these old parts exactly as they were, that the part recovered might be suited to them. They acted ... not by the organic *moleculae* of a disbanded people.

(A reference to contemporary France and to the idea of starting history anew.) Burke's view of relatively recent history was related to a more general interpretation of English history. Citing William Blackstone's 1759 edition of Magna Carta, and quoting from the texts of the Petition of Right (1628) and the Declaration of Rights (1689), all episodes in English history, Burke claimed:

> It has been the uniform policy of our constitution to claim and assert our liberties, as an entailed inheritance derived to us from our fore-fathers, and to be transmitted to posterity... This policy appears to me to be ... the happy effect of following nature, which is wisdom without reflection ... People will not look forward to posterity, who never look backward to their ancestors.[1]

'History wars' played a key role in politics or, at least, political rhetoric for Burke, his opponents, and others. Burke continued, in his *Appeal from the New to the Old Whigs* (1791), to argue that it was his views that were consistent with the Glorious Revolution, rather than those of Whig radicals, most prominently Richard Price and Joseph Priestley. In his sermon 'On the Love of Our Country,' preached at a meeting house in London on 4 November 1789, Price, a prominent Dissenting minister, described the French Revolution as 'glorious'.

Burke, however, claimed that this Revolution was not compatible with the Glorious Revolution, as the Whig radicals argued in their attempt to claim the historical legacy in support of their direction of travel. Instead, he linked the Revolution with the regicide of 1649, the execution of Charles I, a step that had traumatic religious as well as political resonances. Thus, history was not only asserted as a principle by Burke, but also contested as a practice. Burke felt that the events of 1688–9 could only be appreciated in the light of the assumptions to which they had given rise, and he did this to deny contemporary radical attempts to interpret the legacy.

As the French Revolution became increasingly violent and extreme, it became easier in British discussion to deploy the Glorious Revolution against it. Meanwhile, English/British supporters of the French Revolution also became more radical and, as such, had little time for conventional definitions of loyalty, and thus scant reason to refer for justification to the events of 1688–9. Moreover, their stress on universal principles cut across any emphasis on national history.

In order to condemn the violence in France, the Glorious Revolution was commonly presented in England as an essentially peaceful act. This misleading presentation was made possible by a focus on events in England, where there was some bloodshed, rather than their far more violent Scottish and Irish consequences. Moreover, just as William's actions in 1688–9 could be located in a favourable international context, that of opposition to the aggressive Louis XIV of France (r. 1643–1715), and could thus draw on traditional rivalry between England and France, so the international context in which Revolutionary France was judged, that of proselytism and expansionism by the Revolutionaries, was treated in a highly unsympathetic fashion.

Burke wrote in accord with a dominant note in English nationalism, that of a divinely-intended teleological order that gave meaning and impact to past, present, and future. History was shaped for Burke, as for his contemporaries, including his opponents, by purpose, and was far from being an arbitrary assemblage of events. There were also more specific themes. In the presentation of an account of national history, aesthetic and cultural sympathies were closely linked to politics. Burke was not only a supporter of the Glorious Revolution, but also a writer whose engagement with continuity helped lead to a sensitivity to the Middle Ages. Interest in this period from the late eighteenth century, in terms of the medieval development of Parliament and struggle with France, served to counteract the argument about a Norman Yoke. Indeed, the Anglicisation of the Middle Ages was an instance of the continuity and gradual change Burke applauded and asserted as a principle and demonstration of national character.

The execution of Louis XVI on 21 January 1793 led to the use of the annual January 30 Sermon in Westminster Abbey before the House of Lords, the commemoration of the execution in 1649 of Charles I, who was as near as the Church of England got to a saint, to deliver a powerful attack on political speculation. Samuel Horsley, Bishop of St David's, and a supporter of the government of William Pitt the Younger, presented the constitution as the product and safeguard of a 'legal contract' between crown and people, while the obedience of the latter, he argued, was a religious duty.

The outbreak of war with France in 1793, and the move of the French Revolution that year into the Reign of Terror (1793–4) helped to ensure that Burke's arguments had a powerful and continuing public resonance, one that was far stronger than when the *Reflections* were first published in 1790. The French Revolution saw the formulation of a universalist revolutionary ideology, after which the content and language of politics changed radically in France and among radical sympathisers. The universalist proposition, however, was associated with social division, political violence, and French self-interest.

To a degree, this took forward the self-righteousness, shallowness, and social condescension of much of what has been termed

the Enlightenment; a tendency in which the people were generally presented as ignorant, and their beliefs the very antithesis of
those of the enlightened. The peasantry were to be improved in
spite of themselves, and the language employed to describe them
was that used to discuss children or animals.[2] Enlightenment
intellectuals tended to dismiss what they disliked as supersti-
tions, to exaggerate the possibilities of change through education, and to neglect the difficulties of turning aspirations into
policies, the problems of government, the vitality of popular
religiosity, and the disinclination of people to subordinate self-
interest, and their own notions of a just society, to the views and
self-righteousness of others. This neglect helped to produce
frustration and confusion among some radical thinkers during
the early years of the Revolution, and to engender an attitude in
which the creation and defence of a just society through terror
appeared necessary.

This approach was widely unacceptable in England where it
had been found wanting during the Interregnum (1649–60). The
resonance of Burke's arguments, which were to be highly significant in the development of Conservative thinking,[3] as they still
are, was supported by a renewed interest, in revealed theology, in
revelation—Providentialism and Biblicalism—rather than in
apparent natural religious truths. This renewed interest for some
was part of an increased critique of reason, heterodoxy, deism,
and science.

Clerical writers, such as Edward Nares, the largely non-resi-
dent Regius Professor of Modern History at Oxford from 1813
until 1841, took forward Burke's themes. Nares combined a
nationalistic perspective, born of Anglican zeal and hostility
towards foreign developments, with a strong interest in history.
In 1828, he produced an important, three-volume, life of
William Cecil, Lord Burghley, declaring, in the preface, his
determination to link patriotism and Protestantism: 'he prides

himself upon being an Englishman, an English Protestant, a Church of England man, a Divine.'[4] Burghley, Secretary of State and later Lord Treasurer to Elizabeth I, was a key figure in the positive portrayal of that reign. At the same time, more than religion was on offer as a definition and defence of nationalism.

In England, national history and culture, for example, the works of Shakespeare, served to offer an alternative to the Classics as providers of a currency of discussion and reference in an age with a more democratic political and cultural language. The lengthy war with France (1793–1815) proved readily adaptable as the source of exemplary tales, and did so across a variety of genres, including paintings, poetry, sculpture, and fiction. In the 1800s, there was a focus on George III and the constitution, but as an archetype of a legal, popularly-grounded political system that contrasted with that of Napoleon. There was less focus on the power of the ruler in Britain.

The cultural movement of Romanticism, meanwhile, focused strongly on identity with landscape and especially with mountains, as with William Gilpin (1724–1804) and the origin of English tourism, notably of the picturesque. In 1782 he published his *Observations on the River Wye* following with the Lake District (1786), Scottish Highlands (1789), New Forest (1791), and West of England (1798). The linked emphasis on original virtue and the physical environment, in at least the shape of landscape, led to a stress on distinctive features and areas, for example the Lake District; rather than on the more general impact of civilisation. This approach was intellectually matched by the definition of geology as an important and fashionable subject, one that underlined the distinctiveness of terrain.

The political equivalent of Romanticism was an interest in Medievalism, with the latter taken back to consider pre-Roman roots. Thus, Thomas Percy, a grocer's son who sought to show his descent from the medieval Dukes of Northumberland, published *Reliques of Ancient English Poetry* (1765), an edition of old ballads which promoted a revival of interest in the subject. In *Mansfield Park*, Jane Austen described Shakespeare as 'part of an Englishman's constitution. His thoughts and beauties are so spread abroad that one touches them everywhere; one is intimate with him by instinct.' Neo-Gothic novels, such as those of Ann Radcliffe, drew on Shakespearean themes.

So also with history. In his *History of the County of Cumberland* (1794), William Hutchinson, a lawyer, presented the descent of nationhood from Antiquity. A primitive, original virtue was depicted. Beginning with the Brigantes, the powerful pre-Roman tribe in the North, Hutchinson discussed Queen Cartimandua (r. c. 43–c. 69): 'In those days, it was no disgrace, to the bravest people, to be governed by a woman; disgustful effeminacies had not then contaminated the sex.' In contrast, Hutchinson presented Roman luxury, wealth, and manners as bringing corruption and vice. He rejected Roman values as incompatible 'with the general tenor of the Druid administration, the tenets of which were deduced from moral obligation.' Pre-Roman culture was readily praised by Hutchinson who described the Druids as 'an order of men possessed of all the learning of the age,' arguing, as a result, that the people were 'wonderfully enlightened,' with their theology uncorrupted by 'idolatry.' Moreover, also, in contrast to the vice-ridden Romans, Hutchinson saw Roman Britain as subsequently conquered by 'warlike and ferocious bands ... uncontaminated with their vices.'[5]

The Saxons were in general compared favourably with the less attractive Romans and the Normans. In contrast, the Vikings were widely criticised, and, indeed, were termed 'the Vandals of Scandinavia' and contrasted unfavourably with the Saxons by Sharon Turner in his *History of England* (1799–1805). Whereas the Saxons were anglicised and adopted as key elements in the development of Englishness, the Vikings were treated as foreign.

That Scotland, Wales, and Ireland were not parts of the Anglo-Saxon world meant that the last was very much seen as the precursor of Englishness, and thus as different from Britishness. The language of Britishness might be used, but the reality was of Englishness, as a patriotic Anglo-Saxonism meant nothing in Ireland, Scotland, and Wales. The use of the Middle Ages in England was distinctly English not Scottish, not least because the two powers had repeatedly fought each other. Medievalism also offered an opportunity to emphasise hostility to France, as with George Colman the Younger's play *The Surrender of Calais* (1791). This referred to English success at Calais in 1347, not its loss under Queen Mary in 1558, and closed:

> Rear, rear our English banner high.
> in token proud of victory!
> Where'er our god of battle strides,
> Loud sound the trumpet of fame!
> Where'er the English warrior rides
> May laurelled conquest grace his name.

There was an interchangeable Englishness and Britishness at this stage, at least in England. In his *Notes to Accompany Mr. Wyld's Model of the Earth*, a model of the globe displayed in Leicester Square, London, from 1851–62, James Wyld, MP, referred to 'the civilising sway of the English crown.'[6] War was part of the equation. Thus, heroism focused a potent sense of meritorious masculinity, imperial destiny, and a quasi-religious trial and salvation. On the pattern of Rome, there was co-operation between élite and populace in a rapid expansion of imperial power, one that was readily enforced on others.[7]

Within the British Empire, to describe yourself as English was the norm, including for people who by geography rather than ethnicity were Irish or Scots. This still applies to the American usage of England, as noted in *Huffington Post* on 19 December 2012 when it corrected the allocation of West Wales to being part of England. The approach to nationality posed issues for those who were immigrants.[8]

As an added aspect of the primacy of Englishness, there were many cases of upper-class or professional people who were born and lived most of their lives outside the British Isles, with usually the critical exception of having been educated at an English public school, but who still called themselves English. They could be simultaneously English and also Scots, Welsh or Irish, English being their wider identity. Thus, in 1915, the kilt-wearing Scottish general Sir Ian Hamilton (1853–1947) described Horatio Kitchener (1850–1916), whose family home was in Ireland, as the 'idol of England' with no sense of incongruity.[9] While the English tended not to differentiate themselves from Britishness, there was also a crucial multinational character to Britishness. Most particularly, Scots benefited greatly from Britain and its empire. The English essentially called the shots, certainly in financial terms, but the Scots (and Welsh and many of the Irish) largely acquiesced, partly because of the argument of Britishness. Moreover, they could be the first to correct any foreigners who called them 'English.'

That Scotland retained considerable independence within the United Kingdom also militated against political nationalism. It had its own established Church and educational system, as well as a distinctive legal system. Furthermore, in 1885, the Scottish Office and Secretary were created, the first Secretary of State for Scotland since 1746.

Yet, alongside an awareness of distinctive features and a different heritage, nationalism was weak in Scotland in large part due to identification with the idea of Britain and the benefits of the British Empire. There was a re-emergent cultural identity, with kilts and literary consciousness, but no real drive for independence. The religious dimension, so obvious in Ireland, was lacking. Launched in 1853, the National Association for the

Vindication of Scottish Rights pressed for administrative devolution and Cabinet-level representation, but was not explicitly nationalist. The notion of North Britain was rejected by the late nineteenth century, in favour of that of Scotland, but it was an increasingly anglicised Scotland.

Five of the ten Prime Ministers between 1880 and 1935 were Scottish. As in the eighteenth century, the Scots were very heavily represented in the army. Furthermore, Scotland was not only an aspect of imperial Britishness, as with the military, politics, and trade of Scotland, but also a local imperial identity, the same fundamentally as being British and Canadian. Individual careers reflected the significance of British links. William Gladstone, Liberal Prime Minister, born in England to two Scottish parents, retained a Scottish connection, but Liverpool, Oxford, London, and Hawarden in Wales were also crucial places in his life and experience.

Although with important variations of their own, the Scots subscribed to the prevalent Whig interpretation of history. This was a public myth that offered a comforting and glorious account that appeared appropriate for a state that ruled much of the globe and which was exporting its constitutional arrangements to other parts of the world.

For England, this progress was portrayed within a seamless web that stretched back to the supposedly free and democratic village communities of Angles and Saxons applauded by John Richard Green in his *Short History of the English People* (1874). An idealisation of democracy as inherently English was in line with the politics of the spreading electoral franchise. Thus, after the setback of the Norman Conquest in 1066, the successful quest for liberty could be traced to Magna Carta in 1215, and to other episodes which could be presented as constitutional struggles in medieval England, as well as forwards to the extensions of the (male) franchise in 1832, 1867 and 1884, which were presented as arising naturally from the country's development. This assumption about organic change was also long-present in fiction. In *An English Murder* (1951), the lawyer and novelist Cyril Hare referred to 'England, where relics of the past are permitted not only to exist but to influence the present.'

National independence was another theme, with the rejection of foreign control and challenges emphasised, as in the treatment of Henry VIII, the Reformation, and Elizabeth I, for example by J.A. Froude in his influential *History of England from the Fall of Wolsey to the Defeat of the Spanish Armada* (1858–70). The Glorious Revolution was very much to the fore. Captain Montagu Burrows RN, Professor of Modern History at Oxford, wrote in *The History of the Foreign Policy of Great Britain* (1895):

> Happily for the world ... the Revolution of 1688 once more opened up the way to the resumption of the Tudor foreign policy.... Not one word too much has been said in praise of the benefit conferred upon England and the world by the Revolution. From the 5th of November 1688 [when William landed at Torbay] dates the return of England to her old place.... The nation had long been aware of the evils of a departure from the principles entwined with its whole earlier history, and exemplified in chief by the great Elizabeth.[10]

Another prominent historian, Sir Adolphus Ward, argued that the later Stuarts had depressed 'the English monarchy to the position of a vassal state,' while William III was 'one of the most far-sighted of great statesmen'.[11]

The Protestant approach coloured the treatment of the past. For example, the 1815 edition of the *Encyclopaedia Britannica* noted that:

> The reign of Edgar [959–75] proved one of the most fortunate mentioned in the ancient English history. He took the most effectual methods both for preventing tumults at home and invasions from abroad... The greatness of King Edgar, which is very much celebrated by the English historians, was owing to the harmony which reigned

between him and his subjects; and the reason of this good agreement was that the king sided with Dunstan [Archbishop of Canterbury, 959–88] and the [Benedictine] monks, who had acquired a great ascendant over the people. He enabled them to accomplish their favourite scheme of dispossessing the secular canons of all the monasteries; and he consulted them not only in ecclesiastical but also in civil affairs. On these accounts, he is celebrated by the monkish writers with the highest praises; though it is plain, from some of his actions, that he was a man who could be bound neither by the ties of religion nor humanity.[12]

The modern Empire was given a strong and long historical component, by being presented as both apogee and conclusion of a historical process begun with ancient Rome. Architecture reflected this reference to past glory. The neo-Classicism of the late eighteenth century drew heavily on Roman models, but that of the early nineteenth was dominated by Greek Revival. Neo-Gothic was also highly influential.

A sense of national superiority was also reaffirmed through a combination of the notion of the leader of civilisation with the precepts of Social Darwinism, the idea of an inherent competitiveness leading to a survival of the fittest. This approach was seen as a way to explain and thus affirm national success. Social Darwinism led to a view of the nation-state as an organic entity that needed to grow if it was to avoid decline, an inherently aggressive attitude. Racial pride was another aspect of nationalism.

Heroic nationalism was a theme across social classes, and for all generations. Charles Kingsley (1819–75), a clergyman who was Regius Professor of Modern History at Cambridge from 1860 to 1869, wrote a number of historical novels glorifying heroes from the English past. These included *Westward Ho!* (1855), an account of the Elizabethan struggle with Philip II of Spain, in which the Inquisition and the Jesuits appear as a cruel inspiration of Spanish action, and *Hereward the Wake* (1866) about resistance to the Norman Conquest.

In his popular, well-written adventure stories for boys, the war correspondent George Alfred Henty (1832–1902) looked at past as well as present. His historical accounts, which continued to enjoy substantial sales until after World War Two, and which were available in my newly-constructed local public library in the 1960s, included such novels as *Under Drake's Flag* (1883), *St George for England: A Tale of Cressy* [Crécy, 1346] *and Poitiers* [1356], and *Held Fast for England: A Tale of the Siege of Gibraltar* (1892). The last related to the siege of 1779–83, when the state in question was in fact Britain, not England.

This reading of Britain as England was commonplace, a situation that has lasted to the present in England. For many commentators, Englishness and Britishness were as if coincident. For example, the Canadian writer Robert Barr (1849–1912), in his 1904–5 detective short stories about Eugène Valmont, a French detective working in London, frequently treated England and Britain as interchangeable.[13] In this and other cases, the role of interpretations from within the wider anglosphere was readily apparent. Another writer of detective fiction was Ferguson Wright Hume (1859–1932). Born in England to Scottish parents, and brought up in New Zealand, before working in Australia and returning to Britain in 1888, he had an Australian returning to England say: 'We are going to keep Christmas in the real old English fashion. Washington Irving's style, you know: holly, wassail-bowl, games, and mistletoe.'[14]

The focus on England was more general. It was spread by the 'Condition of England' movement, which was linked to the cult of novels that was so strong from the 1840s and which had already been seen in William Cobbett's accounts, as in that, sent from Derby in 1829, of the diet of the poor, ending 'And this is ENGLAND!'. Prefiguring J.B. Priestley, Cobbett was a very English writer who was steeped in English localities and was deeply committed to a geographical Englishness, but was a trenchant critic of the social and political systems.

The English read Sir Walter Scott's novels, both the realist ones set in Scotland such as *Waverley* (1814), and those in England. The latter included *Ivanhoe* (1820), which was set during the reigns of Richard I and John, and *Kenilworth* (1821), a romantic story about Elizabeth I and Robert, Earl of Leicester. Nevertheless, Charles Dickens and other leading English novelists did not tend to engage with Scotland. The treatment of Britain as England was wide-ranging, and almost automatic. For example, the appeal of politics was referred to in Wilkie Collins's *The Moonstone* (1868):

> The guests present being all English, it is needless to say that, as soon as the wholesome check exercised by the presence of the ladies was removed, the conversation turned on politics as a necessary result. In respect to this all-absorbing national topic, I happen to be one of the most un-English Englishmen living.

In 1838, William Wordsworth, writing in his conservative later years, in his *Protest Against the Ballot*, a particularly poor poem, had called on St George to stop the introduction of the ballot. Conservative activism might spread across Britain, but it tended to focus on England. This was the case with the Primrose League, a popular Conservative movement launched in 1883, that enjoyed much support in the 1880s and 1890s for its defence of Crown, social system, and Empire.

Irishness proved an important point of tension, not only in Ireland but also elsewhere in the United Kingdom. The Great Famine of the late 1840s led to the move of about 2–2¼ million people from Ireland, mostly to the USA, although the Irish-born population of Scotland was 207,000, 7 per cent of the total, in 1851, and that of England and Wales in 1861, 602,000 or 3 per cent. The 1851 census revealed that 23.3 per cent of the adult population of Glasgow was Irish born, and that of 1861 showed nearly 25 per cent of that of Liverpool and 5 per cent of London. Irish migrants tended to live in the areas of cheapest rent, which were invariably the most crowded and least sanitary, such as the East End of London. The migrants focused and exacerbated anti-Catholic feelings, and sometimes undercut native workers, as in the Lanarkshire Coalfield in Scotland where they were used for strike breaking and wage reductions. However, outside Lancashire, a violent response was unusual. Moreover, many Irish immigrants did not live in ghettos but were dispersed across working-class areas, a certain number married Protestants, and many emerged into the middle class, all points underplayed in what became a victim narrative. The Scots attracted less attention than the Irish, but, in the 1860s, there were about 40,000 Scots living in London, a figure that rose considerably over the following century.

Across Europe, nationalism became more insistent and socially comprehensive during the nineteenth century, in part due to democratisation, urbanisation, and mass literacy. Technology was also significant, particularly in the shape of the links opened and strengthened by the railway. London newspapers travelled by train. So also did politicians and royalty. In large part thanks to the train, Queen Victoria and Gladstone saw more of Britain and England than George III and Lord North had done, and the population as a whole had a greater chance of seeing them or of associating them with local individuals, sites and events. Thanks to the train, the royal opening of public works could become a regular event. The steamship made crossings to Ireland quicker, safer, and more predictable. In contrast, no eighteenth-century monarch had visited Scotland, Wales, or Ireland, or indeed the North of England. George III, who travelled the furthest in England and never went abroad, including to Hanover, got no further north than Worcester.

A sense of national success and pride was very clear at the close of the nineteenth century, indeed stronger than at the close of earlier centuries. Material and consumer cultures were important in this. Flags, images of Queen Victoria, and scenes of imperial activity were splashed across advertising and the wrapping of goods, from tea and biscuits to new mechanical devices. This pride was expressed in London, a city that is crucial to the narratives as well as complexities of English nationalism, as it was, at once, the imperial capital, the capital of the United Kingdom, and also the dominant city in England, indeed its *de facto* capital, as opposed to being the capital of the kingdom. As yet, despite immigration in the late nineteenth century, the size, significance, international links and ethnic mix of London were not a particular complication for stereotypes of Englishness, even a challenge to English nationalism, as they are apparently are for many today. In the Victorian period and early twentieth century, Whitehall had grand new ministerial buildings, notably the new War Office (1899–1905) and the new Public Offices (1899–1915). The Mall, the redesigned ceremonial avenue from the refronted Buckingham Palace to Trafalgar Square, was finished in 1913 as a memorial to Queen Victoria (r. 1837–1901), whose statue commands the *rond-point* in front of the palace.

This suggested a Britain of traditional power far removed from the creation of wealth. So also did Tower Bridge, built in the late 1880s with Neo-Gothic embellishments. Yet, the bridge was right up to date in terms of technology, with stationary steam engines powering hydraulic accumulators to raise the bridge's road platform. At this point, there appeared to be a confluence of imperial, national, and local; and an ability to reconcile past and future, history and technology. Moreover, Gilbert and Sullivan's 'He is an Englishman!' song (1878), cited at the start of this chapter, nicely captured, in its combination of gentle mockery with real pride, the assured spirit of English nationalism in the late nineteenth century, and the degree to which this nationalism was not incompatible with the fact that, as the Royal Navy, it was the British navy. Similarly, on 29 April 1904,

Winston Churchill, breaking with the Conservatives and declaring his candidacy as a 'Free Trade' supporter backed by the Liberals, asked the voters of North-West Manchester:

> Whether we are to model ourselves upon the clanking military empires of the Continent of Europe, with their gorgeous Imperial hierarchy fed by enormous tariffs, defended by mighty armies, and propped by every influence of caste privilege and commercial monopoly, or whether our development is to proceed by well-tried English methods towards the ancient and lofty ideals of English citizenship.

The following April, Churchill referred in a speech to the 'regular, settled lines of English democratic development' underpinning the 'free British Empire,'[15] again without contradiction.

George Orwell, in 'England Your England,' the first part of *The Lion and The Unicorn: Socialism and the English Genius* (1941), makes little apology for talking about England when, in all but name, he means Britain. Orwell described England as one of the most democratic nations in the world. Yet, the twentieth century brought in a series of fundamental challenges, notably the two world wars; the crises and collapse of Empire; and relative economic decline, with the accompanying social dislocation and political strife. If Empire, Parliamentary democracy, and Protestantism had been particular features of England, whether or not described and defined as Britain, then these factors collapsed or became less distinctive.

Already prior to the First World War, there was a growing tension about the relationship between Englishness and Britishness, and not only in Ireland where a crisis over Home Rule came to a head in 1914. Elected to Parliament in 1890, David Lloyd George, who became a key Liberal politician and Prime Minister in 1916–22, very much insisted on his Welshness, and provided a political edge to an opposition to Englishness in Church and state. There was a strong desire in Wales for English recognition of the distinctive features of Welsh society. The

Cymru Fydd ('Wales that is to be' or 'Young Wales') Home Rule movement, launched in 1886, was for a time very influential but foundered in 1895–6 on the antagonism between the north and south Welsh, symbolised by Lloyd George and D.A. Thomas respectively. Welsh Liberals were bitterly opposed to Church [the Established Church] schools, especially to measures to provide public assistance to them. The 1902 Balfour Act, providing for finance from the rates, passed by a Conservative government, led to non-compliance termed the 'Welsh Revolt,' with county councils refusing to implement the Act. The Liberals in 1904 won control of every Welsh county council, leading the Conservative government to pass the Education (Local Authority Default) Act, transferring the operation of the Act to the Board of Education so that support grants were paid directly to Church Schools. In Wales, religion was crucial to the political equations, and drew on a widespread religious revival in 1904–6. In 1908, Lloyd George was elected President of the Welsh Baptist Union. Welsh disestablishment debates emphasised the Englishness of the Church in Wales and its 'alienness' in a 'Nonconformist land.' At the same time, the key Welsh issues—land (especially opposition to tithes), disestablishment of the Church, and education—could be presented in radical Liberal terms, and thus incorporated in British politics. Disestablishment was passed by Parliament in 1914, although, due to the war, it was not implemented until 1920.

The outbreak of the First World War in 1914 saw the national mission expressed in a way that conflated Britishness and Englishness. Thus, *1588 to 1914. Album-Atlas of British Victories on the Sea. 'Wooden Walls to Super Dreadnoughts,'* written by the Revd J. Featherstone Stirling, Chaplain to the Forces, and approved by the Official Press Bureau, appeared that year. On the inside page appeared 'Signatures of the Brave. A Place for the autographs of officers and men who served Britain by land and sea in the Great

War of 1914,' topping Shakespeare's lines, 'This happy breed of men ... this England.' The text went back to the Saxons and Alfred the Great, and there was a note on Nelson by F. Hallam Moorhouse: 'At this crisis of our destinies, there is no great dead Englishman to whom the nation's thoughts turn so surely and so proudly as to Nelson.' Nelsonian echoes continued, and not only at sea. In its issue of 22 November 1917, the *Times*, describing a mass British tank attack at Cambrai, noted that the commander 'flew his Admiral's flag at the peak of his tank' and sent a message to all his captains on the eve of the engagement which ran: 'England expects that every tank today will do its damnedest!' Again, old nationalism and new technology were linked.

The majority of the British army was working-class and English. In recruiting propaganda, England was used as the norm. There were occasional regional variations for Scotland, Wales, and Ireland, as in 'join an Irish regiment,' but there were no separate propaganda policies for them, just local variations on a theme. Scotland, Wales, and Ireland are large-scale aspects of a picture of a 'multiple polity,' with each, and indeed the Dominions and India, all being important and all coming together to have more or less the same attitudes, at least at the start of the war. During the war, there was an emphasis on non-English nationalism, obviously in Ireland, and to a lesser extent in India. The extent to which new Australian, Canadian, and New Zealand identities emerged during, and because of, the war is a matter of current debate. Most historians argue that this was much less than modern popular opinion, especially in Australia, thinks. For example, the First Battalion of the Australian army thought of themselves as English.[16] At the same time, there was a sense of separate and superior military identity among the Canadians.[17]

The political crises from the 1910s on led to a breakdown in British nationalism in the shape of the loss of much of Ireland. The Catholic, separatist nationalist party there, Sinn Féin, won the majority of Irish seats in the 1918 general election. The Union with Ireland had been greatly weakened by the earlier failure to respond adequately to the Home Rule movement, and by the willingness, prior to the war, on the part of the Conservatives, to countenance Unionist opposition to it. The firm government response to the 1916 Easter Rising by Catholic separatists was also a significant factor in helping Sinn Féin eventually win support among the Catholic population. This response was understandable as Britain was at war and the separatists were in receipt of German aid, like the Bolsheviks in 1917. However, the situation was read very differently by many in Ireland; and that continues to be the case today, and not only in Ireland.

After the First World War, the government initially resisted Irish nationalism. However, in 1920–1, in reaction to guerrilla warfare and terrorism by the Irish Republican Army, the government, seriously over-committed globally, gave way with the Anglo-Irish Treaty of December 1921. Nationalist acceptance of the partition of Ireland was the price for the government eventually agreeing a settlement. The nationalists gained control of what became the Irish Free State, the bulk of the island, which was initially a self-governing Dominion within the Empire, with the Governor-General appointed by the Crown. In 1937, under a new constitution, the state became Eire and the oath of allegiance to the Crown that MPs had been obliged to take under the 1921 treaty was abolished. Vestigial British authority was extinguished by the Republic of Ireland Act of 1948 to which the UK responded with the Ireland Act of 1949. As a distinct new territory, the Protestant-dominated Northern Ireland (most, but not all, of the historic province of Ulster) remained part of the United Kingdom, which became the United Kingdom of Great Britain and Northern Ireland. Another aspect of significant change on the British scale was that the Church in Wales was disestablished in 1920.

There was no comparable disruption in Britain itself. In England, Scotland and Wales, had the General Strike of 1926 led to violence or to a change of government, neither of which was the intention of the trade union leadership or membership, then the political situation in the 1930s during the Depression might have been less propitious. However, although the background was of a rapidly-changing country, the combination of this change with an inherent political stability was notable. The conservatism of the 1920s and 1930s was an expression of a strong view of national identity as inherently traditional or, at least conventional and as opposed to novelty and radicalism. Political calculation also played a role. The threat from Socialism was played up in the 1920s and, to a lesser extent, 1930s in order to destroy the Liberal Party, as the Conservatives correctly assumed that the bulk of Liberal voters would turn to them.

There was a strong cultural counterpart to the political position of Stanley Baldwin, the Conservative leader from 1923 to 1937 and Prime Minister in 1923, 1924–9 and 1935–37. In rejecting, in the 1930s, the Communists, as well as Oswald Mosley's far-Right British Union of Fascists, which he presented as un British, Baldwin stressed national identity, continuity, distinctiveness, and stolid common sense. He did so not to embrace political reaction, but rather to seek an imaginative way to lessen tensions arising from economic change, especially rivalry between capital and labour. Baldwin was photographed with pigs and five-bar gates, helping underline an identification with an image of rural values. This approach proved particularly successful in England, but the Conservatives failed to make a strong impact in Wales.[18] Historical writing and journalism were deployed to emphasise national roots in a way designed to be relevant not simply to the privileged few but to all, a project that had a sound basis in inter-war society.[19] In 1924, Baldwin, addressing the annual dinner of the Royal Society of St George, noted 'a feeling of satisfaction and profound thankfulness that I may use the word "England" without some fellow at the back of the room shouting out "Britain."'

Limits on immigration were an aspect of the understanding of national identities, although ethnic issues were less pronounced politically and socially than they had been in the 1840s-50s—the period of mass Irish immigration—or than they were to become later in the 1960s and, even more, the 2000s and 2010s. However, restrictions on immigration in 1905, 1914 and 1919 testified to a loss of confidence, and there was a widespread low-level racism and anti-Semitism. These could at times lead to violence, but were more commonly a matter of social assumptions and institutional practices, as in exclusion policies for golf clubs or private schools or housing. In comparison with the situation today, there was very little racial co-habitation or intermarriage.

There was a widespread assumption, frequently reiterated in popular fiction, that foreigners were particularly associated with crime and drug-taking, and notably so in London. Detective novels often contrasted rugged English heroes, who relied on their fists, with foreign residents of London, who were generally presented in terms of supposedly undesirable physical characteristics, such as shifty looks and yellowish skins, and as using knives. Alexander Waugh, a London-based novelist (1898–1981), described Soho in 1926 in terms of 'a swarthy duskiness, and oriental flavour; a cringing savagery that waits its hour.' In practice, alongside upper-class criminals,[20] London's key gangsters were the Sabinis, led by an Anglo-Italian, Charles 'Darby,' while the Messina brothers dominated prostitution.

Writing in 1941, George Orwell argued that 'It needs some very great disaster, such as prolonged subjugation by a foreign enemy, to destroy a national culture.' At the same time, he proffered a Baldwin-like account of the current situation: 'The gentleness, the hypocrisy, the thoughtlessness, the reverence for law and the hatred of uniforms will remain, along with the suet puddings and the misty skies.'

There was also very varied ethos and competing visions of England offered in the period covered in this chapter. Behind the idea of a united Empire and a proud imperial heartland, had come that of marked divisions within Britain and England. In large part, these were a consequence of industrialisation and of associated understandings of identity. The change was especially remarkable in terms of the presentation of Britain's regions, and especially in England. The nineteenth century had seen a marked reconceptualisation of older ideas of the North as opposed to the South. The sense of regionalism changed. In his *Historical Maps of England during the First Thirteen Centuries* (1869), Charles Henry Pearson (1830–94) argued that geography was for long the key element. Pearson, earlier Professor of Modern History at King's College, London, and later a Cambridge historian, eventually became a prominent politician in Australia.[21] He suggested that, although 'man triumphs over the elements,' this triumph was essentially a matter only of the previous half-century. Pearson saw geography at work in the earlier divisions of the country's history. He regarded the mountains as 'the conservative element ... in our history,' and observed that the Roman presence was limited in the upland regions—the South-West, Wales, Galloway and Lancashire—and that 'it was precisely these parts where the nationality was unbroken, that afterwards sustained the struggle against the Saxon.' In the civil war of Stephen's reign (1135–54), he claimed 'the Empress Matilda, who represented the not infrequent combination of a legitimate title and an oppressive government' drew her support from the upland west, Stephen from London 'and the commercial towns of the east.' Similar comments were made about the Civil War (1642–6), and then, for the Jacobite uprisings in 1745: 'nowhere, except in the Highlands could Prince Charles Edward have raised an army;

nowhere but in the north-western counties, still only partially civilised, did he find recruits. Our country is so small, that in Cumberland and Westmoreland at least, the hills are losing their old influence.'[22]

This interpretation neatly linked a conventional view of progress through a limitation of royal authority, with a sense that upland areas were socially conservative and politically reactionary. The geographical basis of support for the two sides in the Civil War received (as it still receives) considerable attention and is often related to socio-economic criteria.

In the late nineteenth century, in contrast, the North was associated with industry, and the South with ruralism and pastoralism which were seen as part of English identity.[23] Ruralism and pastoralism remained significant in the twentieth century and, if anything, became stronger. This tendency took a number of forms. One of the most lasting was that of the development of suburbia as a matter of separate or semi-detached houses, each with a garden: indeed with a small front and a larger back garden. In contrast, flats/apartments were seen as inappropriate and as unEnglish. Speaking on the West of England radio programme on 2 January 1939, John Betjeman attacked the slum-clearance schemes of the London County Council, adding 'Londoners, like all English people, prefer to live in a house.' Gardening became increasingly significant as an expression of Englishness.

Suburbia was particularly pronounced around London and was an aspect of the demographic and economic shift from areas in the North, South Wales, and Central Scotland that had, together, been the workshop of the world, to the South-East. This tendency has continued to this day, such that the demographic centre-points of Britain and England have moved southward. This has literally led to a 're-placing' of England, but one that was not widely acceptable across much of the country.

Instead, there were repeated demands for investment in 'the North,' which, in practice, represented redistribution of funds from the South, more particularly London and the South-East. There is a natural conflict within any country between the centre, where power lies, and distant regions, where people feel they do not receive 'a fair share of the cake,' to employ the sort of phrase that makes politics readily comprehensible.

A related, but different, tendency was that of the cult of the landscape that was especially strong in the 1920s and 1930s, with the landscape mainly linked to such Southern features as downland. Conservationists, who had founded the National Trust in 1895, and others drew on a strong sense that change and modernisation threatened national identity, value, and vigour.

The arts reflected these changes without being restricted to them. The Crafts movement developed from the late nineteenth century, in large part as an affirmation of a vernacular, English culture that was worth defending. In music, the positive response to Edward Elgar, Ralph Vaughan Williams, and Percy Grainger was linked to these values and commitments, as was the popularity in painting and fiction of 'authentic,' rather than Modernist, works. The Royal Academy Schools and the Elizabethan timber style of Liberty's department store in London (1924) were characterised by a conservatism greatly at odds with Modernism, while James Bolivar Manson (1879–1945), the Tate Gallery's Director in the 1930s and a painter of flowers, was opposed to Cubism, Expressionism, and Surrealism.

In fiction, there were ruralist writers, such as Henry Williamson, author of *Tarka the Otter* (1927), which I read as a child. In his *Linhay on the Downs* (1938), he referred to 'the harmony of nature,' a central theme in much inter-war culture. In his far more complex poem *Waste Land* (1922), the American-born Londoner T.S. Eliot (1888–1965) testified to the strength of Elizabethan references in English culture when he referred to:

... Elizabeth and Leicester
Beating Oars.

One of the most successful disseminators of the ruralist image
of England was H.V. [Henry Canova Vollam] Morton (1892–
1979). Born in Birmingham and a journalist, he was one of the
most popular writers of his day and was close to many leading
figures accompanying Churchill to the Atlantic Charter negotiations with President Roosevelt in 1941.[24] Based on travel pieces
in the *Daily Express*, Morton's *In Search of England*, first published on 2 June 1927, had two other editions in 1927, three
each in 1928, 1929 and 1930, four in 1931, and appeared in its
twenty-fourth in 1937. It was the most influential of a whole
genre of tour guides to parts of England that were very popular
in the inter-war period. They reflected the possibilities for individual touring created by the spreading ownership of cars, of
which there were about two million by 1939. This process was
linked to the spread of suburbia, but not simply a matter of it.
England was being 'discovered' as a result, as cars and rural bus
services reached many areas not readily accessible by train, while
posters encouraged rail travel for tourism. To Morton, the countryside was integral to national life:

> The squares of London, those sacred little patches of the country-
> side preserved, perhaps by the Anglo-Saxon instinct for grass and
> trees, hold in their restricted glades some part of the magic of spring.
> I suppose many a man has stood at his window above a London
> square in April hearing a message from the lanes of England ... the
> village that symbolizes England sleeps in the subconsciousness of
> many a townsman. A little factory hand whom I met during the war
> confessed to me, when pressed ... that he visualised the England he
> was fighting for—the England of the 'England wants You' poster as
> not London, not his own streets, but as Epping Forest, the green
> place where he had spent Bank Holidays. And I think most of us
> did. The village and the English countryside are the germs of all we

are and all we have become: our manufacturing cities belong to the last century and a half; our villages stand with their roots in the Heptarchy [Anglo-Saxon period].

At the close of the book, the reader, already taken by car to Land's End, and then to the Scottish border, and back to Kenilworth 'in the heart of England,' is offered, in the last, probably in a fictional passage, a rural idyll when Morton meets a vicar who provides an attractive account of timelessness:

> We are, in this little hamlet, untouched by ideas, in spite of the wireless and the charabanc. We use words long since abandoned. My parishioners believe firmly in a physical resurrection. ... We are far from the pain of cities, the complexities. Life is reduced here to a single common denominator ... We are rooted in something firmer than fashion... the newspapers are only another kind of fairy story about the world outside.

Morton's book thus closes with an assertion of faith and a powerful account of an identity of people and place:

> I went out into the churchyard where the green stones nodded together, and I took up a handful of earth and felt it crumble and run through my fingers, thinking that as long as one English field lies against another there is something left in the world for a man to love.

Morton saw the agricultural workers as 'the salt of the earth,' and a kind of well of virtue and character from which the nation received constant refreshment, and called for 'a happy countryside ... guarding the traditions of the race.' An anti-Semite who was hostile to Communism and ambivalent about democracy, Morton left for South Africa after the Second World War. Ernest Barker, who sought national identity somewhat differently in his *The Character of England* (1947), in the cults of the amateur and the gentleman, eccentricity, social harmony, the voluntary habit, and an ability to recreate Englishness, was from a Northern working-class background.

In some quarters, there was also a sense of the occult power of the landscape. This was the case with interest in ley lines, and could also be seen in novels such as Sylvia Townsend Warner's *Lolly Willowes* (1926), with its account of the Chilterns. Similar ruralist themes echoed in the second half of the century, although not continually: in the 1950s, rather than in the 1960s, for example.

Nevertheless, although such themes helped to maintain an idyll of ruralness, they could not preserve the countryside. Morton's vicar indeed is pensive about the lord of the manor: 'poor now as a church mouse but rooted to the land ... When he dies ... I suppose they will sell to pay the death duties and then ...'. Nancy Mitford's 'Uncle Matthew,' a traditional landed aristocrat, in her semi-autobiographical novel *Love in a Cold Climate* (1949), captured the same values, as well as being anti-Catholic. Many landowners indeed sold up, while parts of the countryside were being built over. The organic account of identity is fundamentally ruralist and conservative, although not in the sense of conservatism as the creed of capitalism, indeed far from it. This point is one among many that captures tensions within conservatism and among Conservatives. Indeed, these tensions, like those elsewhere in politics, were and are important to the existence, content, shading and expressing of English nationalism. In *Colonel Sun* (1968), Kingsley Amis, writing as Robert Markham, has James Bond drive past productive farms and ancient forests that would long stand 'as memorials of what England had once been'.

As another very important source and expression of nationality, sport offered a rural account, as cricket, but also urban ones as football and rugby. At the same time, the national pull varied. Within England, Rugby League and Rugby Union divided that sport, while the English Football League started in 1888 with twelve clubs, most in the North-West and the furthest south being Birmingham: there were none in London.

Each of these sports presented England and English organisations as crucial, and not Britain. Thus, England won the football World Cup in 1966. The Football Association is called just that, not the English FA or the FA of England. No change was made to the national structure of organisations, and this was an important qualification of Britishness, although that could be seen in other sporting organisations and events, notably the Olympics.

In so far as Englishness was tribal, it was in part explained in, and by, national sporting events, especially football, cricket, and rugby. Linked to this, it was a question of getting vicarious enjoyment from (or sharing the misery of) team and individual sporting success, with English players above those of the other 'home nations,' a term that was richly significant and one that underlined the sense that the English were one of several.

A strong sense of place was seen with many writers who should not be regarded as ruralist. A self-conscious Yorkshireman, J.B. Priestley had an interest in English character and, in this, valued ordinary people. His *English Journey* (1934) was based on his travels in 1933. Distant from cosmopolitanism, Priestley took forward the realist tradition associated with Dickens, a tradition that was despised by the Modernists. The book was an appeal for democratic socialism, although his compassion did not extend to Irish immigrants. Another Yorkshire writer, the feminist Winifred Holtby (1898–1935) also offered a strong sense of place in her last novel, *South Riding* (1936), a depiction of a Yorkshire community with a headmistress-heroine; as did Daphne Du Maurier (1907–89) for Cornwall. This tradition of writing based on a strong sense of place continued in much of the popular novel writing of the later twentieth century, for example the works of Catherine Cookson (1906–99), which were mostly set in her native Tyneside. A sense of place was also clearly seen and presented in television dramas, for example popular, long-running 'soaps' such as *Till Death Us Do Part*, *Coronation Street*, and *East Enders*.

Change, meanwhile, helped to shape identity, notably the experience of mass unemployment, and associated poverty, in the North in the 1930s. This experience contributed to a strong sense of alienation, and to a political world in which collectivist solutions and the Labour Party took a dominant role. Municipal housing was proportionately more significant in the North.

Alongside accounts of England, there was also the role of Empire and the impact of war. The Second World War (1939–45) underlined the Britishness and imperial character of the unprecedented military effort already seen in the First World War.

At the same time, the war resulted in fundamental changes in the world order, especially in the weakening of the European imperial powers including Britain, even though it was one of the victorious states. These changes took longer to transform Britain itself than they did Italy (where they led to a republic), the Netherlands and France, where the Third Republic was replaced by the Fourth. Nevertheless, the mindset offered by Baldwin and, even more, Morton, was totally displaced in the 1940s. The war, national mobilisation, and Labour government from 1945 to 1951 all led to powerful calls for modernisation and provided many opportunities for modernisers. Citizenship and national identity were redefined, culminating with the 1951 Festival of Britain. However, while traditional notions, whether based on ethnicity, religion or ruralism, no longer appeared relevant, let alone workable, modernisation and social progress proved uncertain, if not inadequate, as the bedrock of identity.

In the 1950s, the Conservative Party that regained power in 1951 sought to reconcile change with continuity, not least by maintaining most of the welfare state and nationalisation of industries introduced under Labour. In 1956, in a last major flourish of imperial power, Britain, in the Suez Crisis, unsuccessfully sought to intimidate Egypt. It had been assumed that Empire could continue after Indian independence in 1947, and there was a determined effort in the early 1950s to keep idea and practice alive. However, government attitudes changed significantly after the Suez Crisis which was correctly seen as a débacle. The following year, in 1957, in his novel *Landed Gently*, Alan Hunter referred to jingoism as doomed, alongside other aspects of the old world, notably the satanic mills and social injustice.

It is however important to add some complexity to this chronology. In particular, as part of a widespread process of seeking to maintain and use empire, either directly or through federalist schemes,[25] Britain remained a major imperial force into the 1950s, and a significant power thereafter. The continued commitment to being a global imperial power helped ensure a reluctance to become involved in the Western European unification offered by the EEC.[26] So also with military power, albeit with the nature of this power being different, and particularly so as clearly secondary to the United States. In the 1950s, Britain still had the second largest navy in the world. Britain also had an enhanced military capability as a result of becoming the third state in the world to gain the atom bomb (1952), followed by the hydrogen bomb (1957). Defence focused on the protection of Western Europe against the threat of Soviet invasion, and Britain played a key role in the Cold War. An active member of international organisations, not least with a permanent seat on the United Nations Security Council, and a key member of NATO, Britain was to display a capacity to act successfully on its own in the Falklands Crisis of 1982, and to return east of Suez from the 1990s, albeit as part of American-led coalitions, especially in the Gulf Wars of 1991 and 2003.

As Empire had played a leading role in British senses of identity, and notably in the Anglo-Scottish partnership, its loss was an important discontinuity. However, younger generations did not feel this. Indeed, this loss constituted an important contrast in the historical memory and imagination between generations, and one that forced the need for new definitions of nationalism and the national interest.

An attempt was made to offer a different identity through the Commonwealth of Nations, which was seen as a way to retain imperial cohesion and strength. Nevertheless, few, beside Queen Elizabeth II, monarch from 1952, took much interest in the Commonwealth, and notably so from the late 1980s; and, as a force for identity, it succumbed to the reality of different concerns and roles. The closing of the Commonwealth Institute in London was more widely symptomatic. Originally the Imperial Institute, established by royal charter in 1888, its name was changed to the Commonwealth Institute in 1958, but following its sale in 2007, it became, in 2016, the home of the Design Museum. After a very brief and unsuccessful history, the British Empire and Commonwealth Museum in Bristol closed in 2009.

The relative decline of Empire was a new context for the expression of national identity. There is a pattern of seeing this as a background for the disintegration of the United Kingdom, and thus for the reflex need for an English nationalism or, alternatively from a Scottish perspective, as an English annexation of Britishness so that it became a little England project. Englishness, indeed, had been a component, almost a cultural definition, of an imperial Britishness, which, until 1947, was quintessentially Imperial. The loss of Empire in South Asia saw the beginning of a different state, a 'Great Britain' that came into being to run a global colonial and trading system that has since disintegrated, or at least to direct a Commonwealth of Nations that has also largely failed. The decline in global power definitely affected the Union with Scotland and the extent of working-class conservatism there. In turn, this 'Great Britain' allegedly morphed into a fretful 'Little Britishness' that was associated in particular, for her Scottish critics, with Mrs Thatcher, the Conservative Prime Minister from 1979 to 1990. Subsequently, Empire and war were downplayed or treated critically as themes in culture and history under 'New Labour' governments in 1997–2010, and multi-culturalism was pushed to the fore when engaging with, and interpreting, both. Indeed, Empire became part of the lost expression of Englishness and Britishness.

As an instance of a new pace and direction of change in the late 1950s, the Macmillan government of 1957–63 sought to modernise Britain by means of more state planning for the economy and applying (unsuccessfully) to join the European Economic Community (EEC); the European Union (EU) from 1993. Indeed, a very different international location for Britain to that of Empire was offered by successive attempts, from the early 1960s, to enter the EEC. Although unintentionally, these were to be an aspect of what became a different society and culture. In the 1960s, the Liverpool Sound, the Swinging Sixties, and the London of Carnaby Street and the mini-skirt created an image far removed from that of the 1950s.

In contrast, there was no interest in English nationalism. Attempts in the early 1950s to argue for an English consciousness, notably with newspaper calls in 1951 for St George's Day to be properly celebrated, had scant resonance.[27] Entry into the EEC in 1973 led to a marked erosion of national sovereignty and to a transfer of powers to European institutions. This properly is the subject of the next chapter.

7

ENGLISHNESS AND THE DECLINE
OF BRITISHNESS, 1968–2018

A parody of Baroness Orczy's play (1903) and then novel (1905), *The Scarlet Pimpernel, Don't Lose Your Head* (1966) was the thirteenth in the series of *Carry On* films. It is from a world that has past. The thirty-one *Carry On* films, which appeared from 1958 to 1992, drew on well-established patterns of music-hall humour, acts, characters and jokes. Aside from gags about sex that would no longer be acceptable, and puns that many today would not grasp, the 1966 film juxtaposed not Britain and France, but England and France. The humour very much drew on national stereotypes. In the St George's Day Special, published in the *Sun* on 23 April 1999, Barbara Windsor, who had made her name in the *Carry On* films, and went on, from 1994 to 2016, to play a major character in *EastEnders*, was listed as one of the '100 reasons why it's great to be English'.

In his 1941 essay 'The Lion and the Unicorn,' which he reworked as *The English People* (1947), George Orwell captured this past world, writing:

> ...there is something distinctive and recognisable in English civilisation. It is a culture as individual as that of Spain. It is somehow

bound up with solid breakfasts and gloomy Sundays, smoky towns and winding roads, green fields and red pillar-boxes. It has a flavour of its own. Moreover, it is continuous, it stretches into the future and the past, there is something in it that persists, as in a living creature... The suet puddings and the red pillar-boxes have entered into your soul.

Yet, in 2018, none of these definitions resonates in the same way, and even talking about 'the English people' would be seen as inappropriate ('non-inclusive') in many quarters, although critics have no satisfactory alternative. Diet has become lighter, so that suet puddings are of the past, while, for breakfast, muesli has largely replaced bacon and eggs, let alone kedgeree or black pudding. Indeed, longstanding traditional dishes have become less common at most meals, although fish and chips still enjoys much favour. What is now traditional is frequently of Chinese or Indian derivation.

Sundays have become less gloomy because changes in law and custom have ensured that Sunday observance is far less common and, indeed, possible, or, even, a term that is understood. Shopping and the television schedules make Sunday much like any other day, and the churches have had scant success in thwarting this. Towns have become much less smoky as a result of the Clean Air Acts of 1956 and 1968 and the linked creation of smokeless zones.

On long journeys, winding roads have been superseded by motorways. If they are now less commonly driven straight through the countryside with scant allowance for its topography than was the case of a generation ago, and are more sensitive to the landscape, motorways and bypasses are still certainly not Orwell's winding roads. Instead, they represent the triumph of town over country, and planning over the particular. As another aspect of change, traditional crops and green fields have been replaced by oilseed rape or maize, or, more seriously and irreversibly, housing. The role of the post has been lessened by the internet and many post offices have been closed. Red phone boxes went faster than pillar boxes. Thus, the manifestations of national civilisation, or, at least, of Englishness, change. A strong presentation of change was captured by Beryl Bainbridge in her *English Journey* (1984), based on a television series in which she retraced the steps of J.B. Priestley's *English Journey* (1934).

A key element in change was the end of the old social and political order as a result of the world wars. This and other shifts had an impact on the Whiggishness that was so important to ideas of a benign Englishness. The narrative was changed and the earlier robustness of the approach was watered down, although important elements of this approach survived into the late twentieth century, and even to today. As another major shift, the teleological progressivism seen with the Whig approach was increasingly interpreted away from constitutional, political and imperial themes. On the Left, it moved to the NHS and social policy, and, on the Right, to a more fractured and often incoherent set of hopes and fears.

Cultural and religious continuity was greatly compromised in the 1960s, notably with the decline in the position, popularity, and relevance of the Established Churches. Americanism and globalisation affected or undermined native styles, whether in food or in diction, with all that they meant for national identity, distinctiveness, and continuity.

Traditional ideas of national interests were challenged, with the building blocks discarded, and the supposed links between them redundant. Established accounts of totemic episodes were attacked. The House of Lords' discussion on 14 July 1986 concerning the forthcoming tercentenary celebrations for the Glorious Revolution, underlined the problems involved in asserting a national history. The situation was very different from the centenary in 1788, and to Edmund Burke's account. Lord

Grimond, a former leader of the Liberal Party, thought the ter-centenary plans provocative to the Irish and, possibly, to Catholics, adding 'that the so-called revolution of 1688 was in fact a *coup d'état*, carried out largely by appealing to religious bigotry, and by treachery.' The Catholic peer Lord Mowbray and Stourton complained because of the subsequent treatment of Catholics, the Earl of Lauderdale because of that of Scotland, and Lord Glenamara (as Ted Short, a former headmaster and then Labour Secretary of State for Education), declared: 'It was a pretty squalid affair. It amounted to nothing more than the ousting of the lawful, rightful king by religious prejudice this ... squalid *coup d'état*.' As Secretary of State, Short had criticised the teaching of English medieval history, arguing, instead, for that of the Vietnam War. Members of the House of Commons, for example the prominent socialist Tony Benn, were also critical of the Glorious Revolution, Benn agreeing on BBC Radio 4 with criticism by the anti-Whig Tory historian Jonathan Clark.

Other views were naturally voiced, and rightly so because, to a considerable degree, 'England's 1688 revolution was a nationalist revolution.'[1] The variety of opinions expressed about 1688 in 1986 and 1988 are a reminder of both the complexity and con-troversial nature of assessing national identity and interests, and the danger of accepting the current scholarly preference for notions of cultural hegemony. Attention to the celebrations of the tercentenary, for example, can well lead to a neglect of con-flicting voices and to a simplification of historical events through ignorance and bias. Nevertheless, the tercentenary proved a damp squib, rather like other national and imperial anniversaries, for example the 250th anniversary of the capture of Quebec from France in 1759. Indeed, the past appeared forgotten, or, as with the bicentenary of Trafalgar in 2005, embarrassing, and this at both the British and the English levels, although not at those of Ireland and Scotland. The emphasis in the second half of the century on national history was not on Empire or war, but on notions of social progress and empowerment. These appeared to be more appropriate as themes for a democratic society commit ted to social welfare. This, however, was not an approach that contributed to nationalism.

The 1960s and what followed had an impact on established senses and institutions of identity and value. This was notably so for traditional aspects and symbols of Englishness, including the monarchy, the Church of England, the legal system, and other institutions. The rise of Scottish and Welsh expressions of identity provided an opportunity for a new focus on Englishness, and not least as Britishness was challenged. Competing ideas of issues of Britishness and Englishness produced possibilities of both compatibility and friction.

In 1957, Rupert Croft-Cooke (1903–79), writing under his pen-name Leo Bruce, felt able to have his sympathetic narrator Lionel Townsend feel 'an Englishman's satisfaction with his national institutions.'[2] That was an approach that, in the 1950s, was to face the withering industry of satire and the pressures of change. At the same time, a degree of confidence in national decision-making, as opposed to that at the EU level, was held to be responsible for support for Brexit, such that only a small minority of 'Remainers' supported a transfer of powers to the EU.[3] Moreover, Pierre Manent, a French academic commentator, pointed out in 2016 that the British political class had not given its soul to the European idea as had its French counterpart.[4] There had certainly been an unwillingness to join the Euro, an unwillingness that remained the case with most of those opposed to Brexit.

A sense of a God-given role implemented in a tolerant fashion had been another key element of a benign Englishness, one employed to differentiate Englishness from what was presented as the intolerance of Catholicism. However, this sense was lost, both with the decline of religion and also with the end of a view of special mission. The belief in a providential role for Empire went with its demise. Since the 1980s, moreover, there has been a troubled relationship between the Conservative Party and the Church of England. A related decline was that of the engagement with the Classics, for the legacy of Rome had been used to provide a vindication of Empire.[5] The rate of change and in particular the end of previous certainties, and of the contact they offered with the past, left confusion and uncertainty for many. To compare modern celebratory occasions, notably the Millennium Dome at Greenwich in 2000 with the Great Exhibition of 1851, was to be aware of a more brittle and questionable optimism about the future.

The weakening of the Church of England was significant to the decline of a common core of nationhood as it had set a tone for many who were not Anglicans. Although many were religious, a smaller percentage of the English population were members of the Established Church. The Church of England's decline, a process that really began, as critics warned, with the Catholic Emancipation Act of 1829, gathered pace in the late twentieth century. The most influential clergyman of the interwar years, William Temple (1881–1944), Bishop of Manchester from 1921 to 1929, Archbishop of York from 1929 to 1942, and Archbishop of Canterbury from 1942 to 1944, had sought to reverse the decline of organised religion and to make England an Anglican nation, and thus to justify the Church of England's claim to speak for it. But, although he strengthened the Church, Temple failed to give England a more clearly Christian character, and his inspiration, as in his *Christianity and Social Order* (1942), of the already-developing role of the Church as a voice of social criticism and concern led to it being seen increasingly in a secular light.[6]

Statistics were scarcely encouraging. There was a widespread and protracted decline in attendance at Easter by Church of

England congregations. In 1931, there had been 2.2 million communicants, but, by 1951, the number had fallen to 1.9 and by 1966 to 1.8 million, and that despite the population rising. Alongside the decline or collapse of faith, however, cultural Anglicanism remained fairly strong.

The Church of England retained a role in education, with many state schools linked to it, albeit not very closely. However, as a consequence of the formation of the NHS, the major role of the Church in charitable functions and the provision of social welfare was largely replaced by the state. The failure in the 1990s of the 'Keep Sunday Special' campaign, one to prevent shops from opening on the Sabbath that was heavily backed by the Church, confirmed the general trend. The decline of Christianity as the glue and purpose of society was readily apparent in the public sphere. No national day of prayer has been held since 1947. Prelates who tried to be both leaders of the Church and guides to their community found it difficult to match the expectations of an increasingly diverse society, which was the fate of Geoffrey Fisher, Archbishop of Canterbury from 1945 to 1961.[7] Separately, the theological diversity of the Church of England created major and persistent problems for its unity, notably over the issues of women priests and, later, women bishops, and over homosexual marriage.

Linked to all this, the overall decline (alongside strength and revival in particular communities), since the 1960s, of Christian religious belief and sentiment has had a major consequence in affecting identity and the past understanding of it in the past, and in the weakening of nationalism. As a collective act, television took over for many. This decline is frequently juxtaposed with the rise of Islam and the strengthening, also due to immigration, largely from Poland, of Catholicism. The net effect is that religious commitment remains strong among part of the population, but, in relative terms, this is far less the case as far as the Church of England is concerned. Moreover, that change very much affects the current of English history, including the position of the Crown and the concept of a distinctive national Church.

The Common Law also suffered a 'political' decline. In large part, this was to do with successive governments' appetite to establish the law and to effect social policy through statute. As a result, the roles of case-law, precedent and judicial decision declined.

Political developments and specific contingencies played a major role in the decline in senses of national exceptionalism, confidence and purpose. A sense of loss can also be linked to a movement away from imperial grandeur. The ranking toward other nations stemming from that grandeur and from victory in both world wars was replaced by a need to define new relationships in less settled times. The positions and pretensions of the United States and the EEC (later EU) each posed questions in this regard.

English/British self-confidence and sense of purpose were also affected. English nationalism in the 1950s and 1960s was in part a gentle pride in nation that was a product of success in two world wars and a sense of superiority born of Empire. Although it was correctly called the British Empire and was as much a Scottish Empire as an English one, while the Soviets and Americans played key roles in defeating the Germans and Japanese, nevertheless it was the English who saw these successes as their achievement and legacy. A theme captured in A.G. McDonnell's comic novel *England, Their England* (1933), was that effortless superiority needed no nationalism. Written by a Scot, the book is about England from the perspective of a foreigner and includes a celebrated portrayal of a village cricket match.

Entry into the EEC in 1973 was seen as important to the debate about nationalism by many at the time, an importance that appeared even more significant with the EU referendum in

2016. In 1962, Hugh Gaitskell, the leader of the Labour Party, then in opposition, warned, in a television interview, that entry into the EEC 'means the end of Britain as an independent nation; we become no more than Texas or California in the United States of Europe. It means the end of a thousand years of history.' He should have been talking about England or Scotland, each of whom could look back a millennium, not Britain, a more recent state, but his comment was still pertinent and was oft-cited in the mid-2010s. In the event, Scottish and Welsh nationalists found much to welcome in the EU, and Euroscepticism was disproportionately English even though it proposed a British nationalism. The difficulty of defending Euroscepticism and British nationalism when there was scant Scottish support for such a policy posed a question mark about the future of Britain unless within the EU as the risk was that Brexit would lead to the dissolution of Britain. That, however, did not match Eurosceptics' idea of a national community, a position hardened by the referendum.

A general sense of national decline, a decline that was certainly there in relative terms, affected confidence, although not equally among individuals and groups. One established narrative, that which is critical of nationalism (and somewhat ambivalent about patriotism), argues that England experienced the loss of Empire, economic decline, and mass immigration; the last affecting England far more than Scotland. To critics, and there were/are many, the response was a descent to the Alf Garnet school of nationalism, as if a good, outward-looking nationalism that was the product of being the best power, turned sour as England/Britain slipped down the league tables, becoming a chauvinism born of fear, outrage and ignorance. Ironically, the results of a poll in January 2018 also revealed considerable Scottish opposition to immigration. Now, to critics, the glowing embers of the new English nationalism had been fanned by fear and powerlessness, and in part by the SNP, into the fears that they see as driving Brexit. For critics, English nationalism of the twenty-first century is a product of perceived failure, social exclusion, mass migration, ignorance and anger. Its Gilbert and Sullivan, Flanders and Swan, charm has been replaced by anger, ugliness and insularity. Thus, nationalism is xenophobia, or is defined accordingly. Nationalism to critics is about 'the Other,' and English nationalism is no exception. Whether Vikings, the French, the Catholics, the Scots, the Germans, or 'Brussels', it is always about the other.

Sport, indeed, an activity in large part conducted by teams playing against other teams, was a key element in nationalism, most notably football.[8] This is the vehicle of nationalism for so many. June 1996 was the date English nationalism was most clearly born in football. England played Scotland at Wembley in the European championships (Euro 96). They had played since 1872, but this was the first time they had ever met in a major international tournament. It served as an eye-opener for England fans to see the sporting divisions between the 'home countries', although antipathy toward English players had been freely voiced by Scots earlier during the 1884–1984 annual series of matches, for example, in 1970 in Glasgow with the chants of 'kill the fucking English bastards' from the enormous crowd. In 1996, there was chaos and Scotland's national anthem, *Flower of Scotland*, was booed by English spectators. The most obvious result of the Euro 96 match was the overnight change in the flag of allegiance for the English, from the Union Jack, as for the English team in the 1966 World Cup, to the Cross of St George. The 1996 match was won by England, the next, a European Championship play-off in 1999, another English success, led to fans fighting in Glasgow. There was no trouble in subsequent matches in 2013 and 2014.

Migration and racism are held to have accentuated the process of changing (and charging) nationalism and redefining 'the

Other.' With respect to nationalism, the question of its relationship with patriotism is dealt with by some commentators by arguing that patriotism is good and nationalism somehow bad. Thus, by critics, the nationalism of 'the ignorant' can be presented as xenophobic, and that of the educated as harking back to the time when Britain ruled the world. Yet, as a reminder of overlaps, alternatively, or in addition, British nationalism is widely treated as good, and English nationalism as bad. The former suggests patriotism and being proud of Britain and its ideals, and showing respect for the monarchy; while English nationalism is associated with trying to get what the Scots, Welsh and Irish have in terms of national identity, and with racism, bigotry, and other unfortunate features, creeping in and muddying the waters, at least as far as the English is concerned. This, however, is all-too-pat and instrumentalist, as well as being an unrealistic distinction.

Critics have also focused on Englishness as a brand of nostalgia, which is one way in which pastoralism as a component of English identity is referred to. This critique leads to criticism of a range of institutions and practices, from the National Trust to television versions of Agatha Christie novels. The National Trust, which has a separate identity and organisation for Scotland, has far more members than any political party, or, indeed, all of them together, and is the largest private landowner in England. The rural aesthetic was also demonstrated by the products sold in National Trust shops and the menus in many of their restaurants. This was a world away from the Britart, Britpop and Cool Britannia of the 1990s. Each were part of the equation, but they were certainly not melded together.

As a reminder of the play of contingency and conjuncture, English identity gathered some more political force after the election of a Labour government in 1997. Earlier Labour governments had either been centralist in attitude or, if they had supported devolution, had not made it a central strand of policy or had lacked the parliamentary strength to introduce it. Indeed, the interest which the Labour governments of 1974–9 displayed in devolution can be explained by their precarious position in the House of Commons and their reliance upon the votes of Scottish National Party and Plaid Cymru MPs in the House of Commons.

In contrast, in order as it saw it, to modernise the United Kingdom, although, in addition, for short-term political advantage, Tony Blair's government was determined to push through a policy of fundamental constitutional change, and, in particular, to alter the relationship between the parts of the British Isles. This policy focused initially on Scotland and Wales. Referenda held in 1997 in Scotland and Wales by the newly-elected national government confirmed what was referred to by Donald Dewar, before, during, and after, the Scottish referendum, as the 'settled will' of its people, won approval for devolved assemblies which were, in turn, elected in 1999. The Welsh Assembly lacked the tax-varying powers of the Scottish Parliament, but the creation of both bodies was a major step. In 1999, powers were also devolved to the Northern Ireland Assembly and to a power-sharing executive there. The debate around 2000 on a federal future was reminiscent of some of the debates about 1910 when federal structures were also discussed. Various leading politicians, including Churchill, had advocated federal reforms as part of a new constitutional settlement; often including a reformed second chamber. Churchill argued for some sort of all-round Home Rule system, so that Ireland would not be different from the other parts of the United Kingdom.

Returning to the 1990s, Scottish nationalism helped to undermine notions of Britishness, at the very least in Scotland. A poll in 2000 revealed that 84 per cent of Scots sampled would describe themselves as Scottish rather than British, which raised interesting questions about the English. In 2002, the *Daily Record*, the most successful Scottish tabloid, urged Scots to support England's opponents in the World Cup, and they did so, much to the shock of the English. The bullying of English children in Scottish schools and the beating up of English students on Scottish streets allegedly became more common, while English students in Scottish universities were described as largely keeping company with each other. A distinctive Scottish viewpoint, frequently opposed to that of London, had been encouraged by the activities of the two Scottish independent television companies: Scottish Television (established 1958) and Grampian Television (1962). Unlike the BBC, they operated only in Scotland, and also took at least half the viewing audience there. On the other hand, in the mid-1990s, 50 per cent of the Scottish sales of tabloid newspapers were of London titles and 75 per cent of those of the 'quality' press. Moreover, James Kelman's novel *How Late I, Was, How Late* (1994), a prominent Scottish literary declaration of cultural self-determination, was published in London by an English publisher and won the Booker Prize, a national award.

By the 2010s, the situation was very different from that in 1997. In the 2015 general election, the SNP won all bar three of the Scottish seats in Westminster. Although it did not do as well in the 2017 general election, the SNP still won an overwhelming majority of the seats then. SNP success is in accordance with the now official presentation of Scottish history and identity, whereby the new National Museum of Scotland in Edinburgh greatly downplays the role of the Scots in the British empire, while the National Library of Scotland also plays up distinctive Scottish aspects in its displays and exhibitions. Thus, the nationalism of the SNP in the present is a different sort of nationalism from the politics of Scottish nationhood hitherto, one drawing on a deep history, but giving it a different goal,[9] which may indeed be what eventually happens in England.

From the perspective of Scottish nationalists, Scotland, which had played a major role in the Empire, had been regionalised from the 1940s, as Britain was no longer seen as a multinational polity, not least because of a smaller cultural engagement by, and with, Scots than in the eighteenth and nineteenth centuries. Instead, the SNP presented Britain as run by England. The rise of Scottish nationalism is in part a reflection of the decline of 'British' endeavours such as Empire and nationalised industries. In January 2018, Nicola Sturgeon, the SNP leader, stated that depending on the likely impact of Brexit on Scotland she would decide by the end of 2018 whether to hold a second independence referendum. The SNP calls for 'independence in Europe'.

Under Blair and thereafter, the pace of constitutional, political and ideological change in England was slower, in part because, unlike in Scotland and Wales, there was no nationalist pressure to assuage or counter. Instead, after the establishment of Scottish and Welsh assemblies, the focus of constitutional change focused on the House of Lords. The monarchy, which consciously maintained its Scottish and Welsh links, was largely excluded from change until the Succession to the Crown Act of 2013 established that the succession to the Crown was not to depend on gender, while disqualification arising from marriage to a Catholic was removed. However, for England, the Labour government elected in 1997 advocated the creation of regional assemblies. These were seen as a counterpart to the Scottish and Welsh assemblies. Furthermore, as in the case of Scotland and Wales, they were presented as legislative and executive bodies designed to match and control the developing pace of administrative devolution. In 1999, eight Regional Development Agencies started work, instructed to prepare an economic strategy for each region. Not under close control by central government, the agencies were under a statutory duty to consult Regional Chambers, non-elected bodies of whom 70 per cent were representatives from all the local authorities in the region.

This process was pressed further in 1999 when, following the Scottish model, the North-East Constitutional Convention, charged with drawing up a blueprint for a directly-elected regional assembly, first met. In practice, this assembly was rejected by a referendum in North-East England. The idea of a regional assembly was seen as expensive and as likely to lead to dominance by Newcastle. Indeed, it exposed the tension within would-be regions as well as their lack of a common identity: the North-East is not just a matter of big industrial cities while Newcastle is particularly disliked by Sunderland and vice-versa. No other assembly was attempted.

Nevertheless, regionalism of a form resumed in the 2010s. Cornish nationalism is certainly growing. It is readily apparent both in local politics, in the frequent display of the Cornish flag, and in bitter complaints about outsiders buying property. The 2017 discussion of redrawing parliamentary constituencies included a seat that spanned the River Tamar, thus incorporating parts of Cornwall and Devon, and this caused widespread anger in Cornwall. This issue underlines the extent to which counties remain more significant than regions, whether the West Country or the South-West. If in Cornwall there is a strong sense of dissatisfaction with national government, it is very unclear that government agencies based in Bristol, or even Exeter or Plymouth, both of which are closer, would be more welcome. The distance from Penzance to Bristol, Swindon, or Bournemouth is great, and accentuated by poor communications, by road and rail, and the latter three cities look more to London than to Devon, let alone Cornwall. In the South-West, shared economic interests are limited, and there is little sense of a cultural or political consciousness that can define and unite a region. Cornwall also has a 'chip-on-the-shoulder' account of being wronged, both in the past and in the present, one that generates a degree of identity by animosity.

In geographical terms, the regional situation is even more obscure elsewhere. To take the Midlands, where two separate regions, West and East, are often discerned, it is unclear how far counties such as Cheshire, Derbyshire, and Oxfordshire should be seen as integral to the Midlands, or as transition zones to neighbouring regions. The East Midlands north, and even immediately south, of the River Trent can be seen as part of the North, Oxford is increasingly a commuter base for London, while Cheshire is as much part of the North-West as of the West Midlands, and Derbyshire of the North as of the East Midlands.

In the South-East, there is the bagel problem: London is central to it, and without London it is unclear how far the constituent parts have any identity or unity. Yet London and the South-East, if established together as a distinct governmental region would be far more populous and wealthy than any other. This might lead to an inherent instability in the process of regionalisation.

The problems posed by the regional perspective was captured in the mid-2010s by the idea of regional mayors, a concept that captured the incongruity of the manner and method of regional devolution in England in recent years. While the concept gained traction in some areas, such as Greater Manchester, the West Midlands and the Solent, in marked contrast, in East Anglia several districts opted out, while in Devon there was considerable and successful opposition.

The regional dimension is not just a problematic one politically. The West Country, London or the West Midlands, and the outer South East, have more people than Wales, Scotland and Northern Ireland respectively. Nevertheless, they receive less attention in coverage of national history, or, generally, with the conspicuous exception of London, press attention. Historians match this neglect.

Essentially for reasons of political calculation, in the shape of the fear that it would be dominated by the Conservatives, the alternative to regionalism, a body for England as a whole, met no favour from the Labour government. Instead, in 1999, it was the Conservative leader, William Hague, an Englishman, who suggested that, when English matters came up for debate in the House of Commons, they should only be debated by English MPs. He did not press on to advocate English autonomy, let alone sovereignty. However, his was an image of England very different to that of regional assemblies.

This approach reflected what was termed the 'West Lothian question,' by which Scottish, Welsh and Northern Irish MPs could vote, and thus legislate, in Westminster for England, while knowing that the legislation would not be applied in Scotland, Wales and Northern Ireland. In 1977, in a warning against devolution, Tam Dayell, Labour MP for West Lothian, a *perpetuum mobile* of parliamentary activity, had asked:

> For how long will English constituencies and English Honourable Members [MPs] tolerate ... at least 119 Honourable Members from Scotland, Wales and Northern Ireland exercising an important and probably often decisive effect on English politics while they themselves have no say in the same matters in Scotland, Wales, and Northern Ireland?

The failure of the 1979 Scottish and Welsh devolution vote in Parliament followed by the Conservative dominance in 1979–97, and then by Conservative weakness in 1997–2010, ensured that the West Lothian question was not to the fore. The issue was raised in the Conservative Party conference in 1998, but Hague did not wish to take any steps that might jeopardise backing in Scotland where the Conservatives were in marked decline.

Indeed, English nationalism as an explicit political force, was then largely associated with mavericks. A good example was Garry Bushell, a London-born newspaper columnist and Oi music figure. From the International Socialists (later the Socialist Workers' Party), Bushell moved to write for *The Sun*, *Daily Star*, and *The People*, and appeared on television. A critic of the EU and of unfettered immigration, Bushell presented himself as English, not British, and campaigned to have an English Parliament and St George's Day recognised as a public holiday in England. In the 2005 general election, Bushell won 3.4% of the votes, 1,216 in total, in Greenwich and Woolwich for the English Democrats Party, their best result that election. This was not the best basis for an electoral triumph, and Bushell somewhat lacked leadership potential.

He was not alone. Founded in 2002, the English Democrats, which presents itself as an equivalent to the SNP, had only 2,500 members in 2015, which certainly does not match the SNP. Its greatest success was to win the mayoral election for Doncaster in 2009, having received 16,961 votes in the first round and, with preference transfers, 25,344 in the second. In 2015, Veritas, a party formed in 2005 following a split from UKIP, merged into the English Democrats. Veritas made opposition to immigration and the EU its key issues. In the 2005 election, it fielded 65 candidates in England and Wales, polling 40,481, with the best result, that for the leader, Robert Kilroy-Silk, in Erewash, being 2,957 votes (5.8%). Poor results led to division and resignations, with a new party, the Popular Alliance, formed as a result in 2006. Subsequent Veritas election results were pathetic. Another flop was the Freedom Party (2000–6) which, in 2004, helped found the English Lobby, a body pressing for an English Parliament and the recognition of St George's Day.

None of these parties matched UKIP in scale or ambition. Founded in 1993, in succession to the Anti-Federalist League (1991–3), and related not to devolution but to a political trend seen more widely in Europe,[10] it had, in November 2016, 32,757 members as well as 20 members of the European Parliament and 253 councillors. This body was the one that helped affect Conservative policy in the 2010s, possibly, as a result of a lack of grip by the Prime Minister from 2010 to 2016, David Cameron, indeed disproportionately so. Possibly that is only clear in hindsight, although Cameron's approach was mocked at the time. On the cover of *Private Eye* for 24 January 2013, Nigel Farage was shown outside No. 10 from which a bubble comes: 'Bloody UKIP, coming over here and taking our jobs.' Moreover, Conservative politicians (and some Labour ones) had been pressing for a referendum for a while, for example, in 2003, on the draft Constitutional Treaty on the Future of Europe. This pressure was strongly opposed by the Blair government.[11]

UKIP won 3.1 per cent of the vote in the 2010 general election, a percentage that would have helped the Conservatives in their unsuccessful quest for a majority of the seats. UKIP then won 12.6 per cent (and over 14 per cent in England), nearly 3.9 million votes in total, in that of 2015, when about one million voters deserted Labour for UKIP. Instead of winning essentially discontented Conservative votes in the South, as had been anticipated, and indeed greatly feared by the Conservatives, UKIP, in that election, showed that it had considerable traction in Labour's working-class strongholds in the North and the Midlands; although not in Scotland. This traction was unexpected and counterintuitive to many commentators, as they had seen UKIP as a right-wing movement born from divisions within the Conservative Party over Europe and therefore most likely to win votes from the Conservatives. Indeed, UKIP did, helping in particular to lessen the Conservatives' hold over many traditional supporters, especially much of its working-class support and many older voters. This working-class support had proved important to Thatcher's electoral victories in 1979, 1983 and 1997. Nevertheless, in 2015, UKIP took many Labour votes, squeezing Labour majorities and coming second to Labour in many Northern constituencies. It was as if the working-class vote had split, not, as under Thatcher, between a Labour majority and an important Conservative minority (a minority still there to help Major in 1992), but now between Labour and UKIP, helping Cameron in 2015, not least by drawing off votes that might otherwise have gone not only to Labour but also, notably in the South-West, to the Liberal Democrats.

However, UKIP's success, not least among working-class voters, did not extend to winning seats in the North then or in the subsequent 2017 general election when its vote collapsed. Subsequently, the party was divided in a chaos of personality struggles and policy divisions. The maximum number of UKIP MPs was two, which was shortly before the 2015 general election, and fell to one as a result of that election, and to zero after that of 2017. It was unclear, for a while, whether UKIP was a harbinger of a right-wing populist movement able to span social divides, or whether it would flicker out, unable to confront the electoral exigencies of the 'first-past-the-post' system, as well as serious weaknesses in its leadership and organisation. In the event, the 2017 election saw UKIP collapse. This was very different from the situation in 2016 when Nigel Farage of UKIP claimed that it would take another one million votes from Labour at the next general election. However, alongside dire leadership, the structures and planning of UKIP repeatedly have been found wanting. By late 2017, membership had fallen to fewer than 25,000 and was falling by close to 1,000 a month. UKIP appears to have been a short-term factor that enjoyed particular and, indeed, undue weight at a specific conjuncture. At the same time, it is possible that similar movements may recur in specific conjunctures, and not just on the Right. Indeed, the upsurge of support for Jeremy Corbyn, although within Labour, can in part be seen in this light.

UKIP did not present itself as an English nationalist party. It sought to be British and it did not only win votes in England, although that was where its support was overwhelmingly concentrated. Indeed, Farage's attempt to campaign in Scotland was unsuccessful. Separately, there were right-wing extremist parties, such as the British National Party (BNP) and Britain First, which was founded by former members of the BNP in 2011, that called themselves British rather than English.

The West Lothian issue came to the fore in the 2010s when it particularly troubled Conservative MPs. In 2012, the government established the Commission on the Consequences of Devolution for the House of Commons to examine the question. English Votes for English Laws (EVEL) was a key issue. Reporting in 2013, the Commission recommended that legislation that affected only England should require the backing of a majority of MPs representing English constituencies. The enabling legislation passed the Commons in 2015, despite strong opposition, notably from the SNP. In one light, this gave England a veto rather than a voice, but, certainly up to now, the measure has not enhanced England's voice in Parliament.[12] Linked to the referendum, Cameron in 2014 also proposed a wide-ranging constitutional settlement designed to help keep Scotland in the United Kingdom; but, looked at differently, this was one of the many passing enthusiasms he failed to sustain. Certainly, no legislation was passed to assuage Scottish concerns.

Devolution for Scotland, Wales and Northern Ireland apparently provided the opportunity, as well as the need, to recover an English identity, and may well do so in the future. Scottish nationalism certainly challenged the situation that being English was seen around the world as synonymous with being from the United Kingdom or Britain, a definition that had been under increasing challenge in recent decades. This recovery appeared to be most in the interests of the English, by which term was understood the inhabitants of England, and not some ethnic group. Indeed, accusations of racism did not really capture the connotation of Englishness. Nevertheless, the idea of an English nation gathered pace, albeit at a far lesser rate than its counterparts. On

24 September 2009, BBC Radio 4's flagship *Today* programme (one of the '100 Reasons' cited in the *Sun* on 23 April 1999) referred to 'our devolved nations,' an approach that, in noting the existence of Scotland, Wales and Northern Ireland as nations, asked the question of what the English entailed.

An English identity might lessen the divisions, probably acute divisions, that would stem from regional governments and assemblies; both the difficulties that might stem from the creation of such bodies and their subsequent rivalries over policy, funding, and maybe borders. Furthermore, such an identity could provide a representation that could stand alongside, even compete, with those of Scotland and Wales in order to give due weight to English interests.

The implicit strength of English identity is indicated in a parallel to the position, past and present, of England within Britain, by the limited role of regional identity in the most populous and economically dynamic part of England, the South-East which had pulled away from the rest of the country from 1991.[13] In response to Brexit, there has been talk of separate statehood for London. On 22 July, a YouGov poll claimed that one in nine Londoners wanted independence, while a quarter favoured a London parliament with powers similar to the Scottish Assembly. Such talk failed to gain traction, and has no real political prospect: as ever, it is instructive to ask what process would make a particular change possible and how and by whom it would be implemented.

This situation is linked to the role of national economic and commercial policies, trends and products, as well as national practices and institutions. All are particularly effective in the South-East. Indeed, to critics, they are overly defined by the South-East. Moreover, to critics elsewhere, there is the question whether the South-East's understanding of the nation and the national is overly limited and partial. An American now naturalised in England and living in Bath observed the strength of the division between North and South, adding: 'I often have the impression that my friends living in London and the South-West think of Wales and Scotland—which are even further afield—as quaint, rather unusual countries that have little in common with life as it is lived in England.'[14]

Meanwhile, cultural change continues to be pronounced. Whereas, in the 1930s, a popular middle-brow voice emphasising national roots for all had a resonance across England, that is less the case today. Yet, alongside differences within England, it, like Britain as a whole, is affected by a degree of homogenisation at the international level, linked to globalisation, Americanisation and consumerism, and for some to Europeanisation. These are aspects of the incessant nature of change and of unprecedented transformations that contribute, for many, to a strong sense of discontinuity and disruption, while others welcome and, indeed, contribute strongly to them. At the same time, Britishness continued to be emphasised. Thus, the opening of the London Olympics in 2012, a ceremonial which won strong plaudits from a wide cross-section of society, neatly straddled English/British themes in the economy, society, culture and politics. This was notably so with the depiction of the Industrial Revolution and the National Health Service. The Olympics were a British occasion, largely, but not exclusively, based in London. Cameron framed them as a patriotic occasion and a cause for renewed patriotism.

Nationalist expressions, in various forms, are correctly presented as in part a populist response to the rate of change. Yet that explanation does not end the debate on the question of national identity, for it would be too reductionist were nationalism to be described simply in this fashion.

There are also different nationalisms at stake within England (as within Britain), even if each can caricature the other, as in 2017 when David Marquand argued that Brexit drew on 'myths, memories and rhetoric' that 'for centuries' had 'transmitted a vision of Englishness of extraordinary power,' a 'profoundly reactionary vision ... the England of Shakespeare, [Enoch] Powell, parliament and the trooping of the colour' [capitalisation as in original]. He contrasted this with 'a second England, sustained by a second vision of Englishness,' that of the Peasants' Revolt, Milton, Paine, the Chartists, and the suffragettes. The EU referendum was seen as a defeat for this second England because 'the leavers had the better tunes. They spoke to the heart.'[15] The son of an academic and former Labour MP, Marquand, a politics academic and a former Labour MP (1955–77) and Chief Advisor to the President of the European Commission (1977–78), a Social Democratic Party politician and then a Blairite, who is an exponent of a federal Europe,[16] was scarcely likely to find much sympathy with what he presented as the alternative viewpoint; but his characterisations were of interest. Shakespeare becomes, for Marquand and others,[17] the exponent of a misconceived and anachronistic 'hymn to England as a "precious stone set in the silver sea"', and not, for example, the pointed critic of the harshness of the social system in *King Lear*, or the misuse of power, as in *Measure for Measure*.

Like the Eurosceptics he criticises (and mirroring the Brexiteers), Marquand draws energy from those he dislikes almost viscerally and presents his own account as normative and paradigmatic. That he is a former academic only appears to ensure that the language employed is somewhat more sophisticated (or modish) than the norm. Maybe, however, all commentary is inherently political, and the institutional and conceptual barriers that historians have tried to define in order safely to practise a would-be panoptic vision are themselves flawed and false.[18]

Coming closer to the present, history becomes memory. It seems familiar, and is, but that can be misleading. Present memory swallows past complexity, and we come to the present without a sufficient understanding of the decades at play. And so with a history that is overly consumed by the politics of 2014–18, notably Brexit (but also the Scottish referendum), and without sufficient measured consideration of what came earlier. The context was crucial, but that was a matter of the context offered by the past and the context of the present. Thus, it is not clear that the journalist Andrew Marr was being helpful when, in 2017 at the commemoration of the erection of an Orwell statue at the BBC, he suggested that Orwell would have voted for Brexit; an ahistorical remark, albeit an interesting one. In practice, Orwell favoured a socialist United States of Europe. As another example of an unhelpful historical analogy, Jacob Rees-Mogg referred in 2018 to the proposed transition period as 'a Norman Conquest' that would make Britain a 'vassal state'.

The Brexit vote was certainly both the product of a divided society and divisive. On a high percentage rate for the UK, 72 per cent of the electorate, just under 52 per cent voted for Brexit, although London, Scotland, graduates and the young voted strongly for Remain. Although the general perception is that working-class voters in the North were responsible for Brexit, one frequently accompanied with pejorative comments[19] (their Scottish counterparts voted Remain), the vote in the South was more important due to the number of voters there. On the national scale, a majority of homeowners who had no mortgage voted for Brexit, as did social and council tenants, whereas a majority of private renters and of people with mortgages voted Remain. Polls suggested that 96 per cent of UKIP voters in the 2015 general election and 58 per cent of the Conservative voters voted Brexit, compared to 37 per cent for the Liberal Democrats, and 25 per cent for the Greens. 53.4 per cent of the English vote was for Brexit, but only 38 per cent of the Scottish and 44.2 per cent of the Northern Irish.

In 1975, the Wilson government was concerned that Scotland and Northern Ireland would vote not to stay in the EEC while

England and Wales voted to do so. In the event, all the 'nations' of the United Kingdom voted then to stay in. What concerned Wilson happened (albeit in reverse) in 2016.

It is naïve to imagine that it is only Brexit supporters who pursue their own nationalist account and are liable to false consciousness. The same is also the case for those offering other approaches to British or English identity and history, and, indeed, the European equivalent. President François Mitterrand told the European Parliament in 1995, 'Nationalisme, c'est la guerre,' but that presentation of political virtue and vice was an amusingly dishonest approach given not only French policy but also the particular supra-nationalism of the EU. Ironically, both the supposed English nationalism decried by Marquand, and the one he favours, cut across the myth entailed in a depiction of Europe as an integrationist project resting on a common history and culture. In 2007, when Germany held the Presidency of the EU, Angela Merkel suggested a standardised history textbook, but none was produced. Instead, a small set stock of figures and episodes were thrust to the fore. Erasmus, the early sixteenth-century Dutch humanist writer, is uncontroversial, but Charlemagne, who, with his coronation by the Pope at Rome in 800, launched what was to be called the Holy Roman Empire, was also a brutal opponent of the Saxons, responsible for the death of large numbers of them, as well as having his name adopted by the SS for a division of French collaborators.

The established EU narrative was hostile to populism well before the 2016 referendum, and the latter should not be allowed to determine and dictate the entire debate. In March 2013, Jean-Claude Juncker, Prime Minister of Luxembourg from 1995 to 2013 and President of the European Commission from 2014, gave an interview with *Der Spiegel*, in which he used the First World War as his point of reference for a discussion of the situation in the EU during the fiscal crisis. In response to the disparate national responses to that crisis, Juncker claimed that circumstances were very similar to those of a century earlier as the war neared. He argued, moreover, that, despite the avoidance of large-scale conflict in Europe since 1945, the issues of war and peace there had not been laid to rest. Juncker also argued that sentiments had surfaced that it had been thought had been relegated to the past.

Thus, Juncker offered the convenient dichotomy of Euro-federalism or chaos. Transnationalism is deployed to typecast the EU's critics as negative and as grounded in a (misplaced) nationalism that draws on history, an approach taken in 2017–18 toward Hungary and Poland. Such arguments make it appropriate to consider populism, to which we turn in the next chapter.

8

POPULISM

other ruffians as their fancies wrought
With selfsame hand, self reasons, and self right
Would shark on you, and men like ravenous fishes
Would feed on one another.

Shakespeare, in one of his generally-agreed upon contributions to the often-overlooked play *Sir Thomas More*, was in no doubt about the evils of populism when referring to the xenophobic May Day riot in London in 1517. He depicted mobs in action in several plays, most memorably *Julius Caesar* and *Coriolanus*, and also in his lengthy presentation in *Henry VI, Part 2* of the 1450 Jack Cade rebellion, a serious, but ultimately unsuccessful, challenge to government power most famous for Shakespeare's often-misquoted line about starting by killing all the lawyers.

Discussion of populism plays a major part in the current assessment of English nationalism, and generally with a highly critical tone. Although the historical dimension is not welcome to many, such discussion is an aspect of longstanding debates—philosophical, political and literary—about the value and values of democracy and democratisation. These can be traced back to

165

the Classical world, more particularly to the constitution and politics of Athens and Rome. It became newly urgent in the nineteenth century, with controversy focusing on the liberal agenda of an expansion in the male franchise. The nature of both authority and power in this developing context became matters of concern to critics. They were worried about the policies that would emerge and concerning structural changes in society, namely that those without a due weight in the community would use the vote in order to redistribute wealth to their benefit; and to the loss not only of property-owners but also of the greater good and goods of society.

At the same time, such populism appeared necessary to governments variously seeking to avoid a repetition of the radicalism associated with the French Revolution (1789), to incorporate subject peoples into imperial or quasi-imperial structures, to do the same for nation-states, not least in order to provide a return for the duty of military service, and as a corollary to the extension by states of universal education. A new social contract was offered; one, in particular, in which power and education were secularised and extended, and therefore held as somehow likely to restrain the risks of popular radicalism. In Britain, populist techniques were part of élite strategies to tame democracy.[1]

In turn, differing strategies of democratisation were put forward in the twentieth century. In part, the interests of the working class were foregrounded in order to advance brutal ideological views, which was the reality of Communism. In part, there were arguments that social welfare was the just reward of the working class. In part, there were determined attempts to win the working class from Communism, attempts focused on full-employment policies and also linked to Christian Democracy in Europe, to the social welfarism variously of the Attlee governments in Britain (1945–51) and of Catholic social policies in Europe, to post-1945 land reform in Japan, and, to a degree, of the passage of Civil Rights measures in the United States.

All these measures were populist in that their rationale rested on representations of popular, more specifically so-called working-class, interests. They were not, of course, truly populist in that many widely-held views were ignored, although generally implicitly rather than explicitly. This was particularly so of popular concerns about immigration, social and cultural radicalism, and crime. Indeed, there was a strong anti-populist nature to the development of twentieth-century democracy, and especially so in reaction to the political dangers allegedly posed to liberal capitalist states. This anti-populist nature tended to be downplayed, but it was very much part of the practice of government and the law and, frequently, of systems of checks and balances, or what were presented as such. Extremism was defined not in accordance with changes sought by government but as an aspect of those that were not sought. Such measures fostered the growing unpopularity of government, which from the 1980s helped to precipitate a crisis in established political parties, breaking long-established patterns in government, including in Canada, Israel, Italy, Japan and, more recently, France. Arguably, Thatcherism in Britain was part of the same process as it explicitly reflected the character of recent Conservative governments, notably that of Edward Heath in 1970–4, as well as of Labour. There was also the challenge of the restructuring of politics after the Cold War, as well as the issues posed by referenda, as in rejections of EU convergence and, eventually, membership.

The ambiguity in the relationship between democracy and populism is taken further at present because of the extent to which populism has become an analytical and rhetorical term. Indeed, there is the danger that, as with the discussion of the history of English nationalism, and related to it, presentism will dominate the question and that, in addition, it will become an aspect of America's culture wars. Populism can become a code word for criticism of President Trump, or Brexit, or much else, in order both to justify hostility and to provide a supposed parallel between what are, in practice and theory, generally very different movements and events. This process was taken further by stirring Marine Le Pen into the pot to provide a form of guilt by association. Populism thus becomes an equivalent to early-modern usage of the term the 'mob,'—itself a term of questionable meaning.

Discussion of populism is moreover marred by a lack of precision. Is it just any popular movement, or a particular kind of popular movement? Can populism be divided into opposition that is approved of and that is not: for example between Sanders and Trump, or between Macron and Le Pen in France, or between Corbyn and Brexiteers in Britain? Is populism by definition irrational (the modern opiate for the masses) or can it be a legitimate expression of the material and social self-interest, and cultural and ideological identities, of substantial sections of the electorate? And what is the relationship between populism and democracy, and between populism and 'majoritarianism'? If Brexit achieves 52% support in a referendum, does that give it democratic legitimacy or disqualify it as 'populism'? How far would the answer to its alleged populism have been different had it won 48%? This is a question that is more generally pertinent. Are critics really objecting to the prime notions of democracy, those of one person one vote and, also, of the legitimacy of opposing points of view?

In the aftermath of the Brexit referendum, some Remainers were doing exactly that. Possibly that was not surprising given that the EU structures and philosophy are fundamentally anti-democratic, and certainly explicitly opposed to populism; but that is not a satisfactory interpretation. Instead, it is more plausible to suggest frustration with what appeared irrational and destructive, and was therefore judged in a pejorative fashion. The EU referendum itself was a populist modification of traditional parliamentary sovereignty with consequences for both British and

English politics. Brexit has certainly affected how English nationalism and populism are understood.

What is a monolith to outsiders, whether English nationalism, opposition to the EU, or whatever, was far from it to those in the know. Moreover, this argument about, and against, populism can become a form of criticism in terms of the standard left-wing notion of false consciousness, namely that people, especially the working-class, allegedly do not, or cannot, understand their true interests because they are supposedly blinded by manipulation in the shape of being led to support foolish ideas. This notion is not restricted to the Left. It has also been identified with Fascist criticism of democratic systems and with critiques of capitalist economies and, especially, of the role of advertising. Another such argument is that deindustrialisation has led to a breakdown of working-class communities as an aspect of a larger social crisis.[2]

Populism can thus be treated with contempt and/or criticism and/or considered as a consequence of failure. Indeed, there is a particularly strong linkage in the case of criticism of religious beliefs, notably as superstitious, an approach that linked some eighteenth-century *philosophes* to later Marxists. The use of language to make a political argument that suits the speaker is very much at issue. Aside from this political and rhetorical convenience, there comes the glib tendency to lump together events and movements for reasons of convenience and in order to make an argument. Journalists and academics are particularly prone to this tendency. In addition to convenience, this tendency often asserts and implies crude explanations of populism. In doing so, it reflects often simplistic and self-serving notions of history, time and causation, notably stadial theories (history through a pattern of stages), as well as explanation in terms of a supposed *zeitgeist* or spirit of the age, or, conversely, with reference to apparently immutable socio-economic tendencies. These instrumentalist and reductionist accounts, for example populism as a response to globalisation, both rob time of contingency, and humans of thought, intention, evaluation and free-action.

Far from new, populism therefore is a concept and a term redolent of past and present thought and controversy about democratisation, and notably as controversy was mounted in particular environments, variously national, political and chronological. There is no reason to believe that the present and future will be different from the past in this respect.

Employed critically, the term populism fails to take adequate note of the electorate's priorities, concerns and reticence about policies where it has reservations about social change with which, in contrast, elites are comfortable, as they are usually best-placed to profit from it.[3] Over the last three decades, *soi-disant* elites in national and supranational bureaucracies, the legal profession, academia, and the traditional print media exemplified by the *New York Times* and the *Financial Times*, appear to have thought that it is desirable to make progress on agendas that irritate large parts of the electorate, and there is no sign that attitudes have changed.[4] This form of political arrogance is very dangerous because it sets up the circumstances where an irritable part of the public considers itself to be both ignored and patronised. In Britain, as elsewhere, this is manifested by local public sector elites speaking to local communities in an argot that they neither understand nor appreciate, and evincing a sensibility that is remote from the local communities that they in theory serve; a situation that can readily be extrapolated onto the national scale.

Discussion of populism today does not necessarily offer a conclusion that handles, still less explains, change in populism through time. Moreover, continuity in thought, rhetoric and/or action, is not the same as similarity in causes, contexts or consequences. Around the world in the 2010s, free-market capitalism and the related politics are under attack, and to a degree not seen since the 1970s. The attacks come from governments, in the shape of the cult of control, growing regulations and redistributive taxation; from within societies, notably with the censorship provided by what is construed as political correctness and the politicisation of higher education, from the replacement of the rule of law by the use of a readily-constructed law to pursue political and governmental agendas, from the conviction that popular views, norms and cultural preferences somehow should trump liberties and long-held values; and from the rise, in some states, of autocratic practices and theories of government. Whether in China or Turkey, these autocratic drives consciously reject the concepts, language and methods of liberalism. These elements are each significant and require mention as part of an assault that is at once general in its intent and consequences, and specific in its manifestations. These, indeed, are cultural clashes, as were predicted in the late nineteenth century in the face of mass urbanisation and the development of populist politics.

There is another and highly unattractive dimension to populism that has attracted insufficient attention. This is the extent to which liberty is under attack in the shape of the threat to national societies from imperialising powers drawing on narratives seeking popular endorsement. The present manifestations are readily apparent in the case of China and Russia, but these do not exhaust the instances of pressure brought upon threatened peoples. In the case of both Russia and China, history is held up as an excuse for expansionism, and by government and public alike. In contrast, the liberal tradition of national self-determination, one strongly pronounced from such nineteenth-century causes as Greek independence and Italian unification (both of which provoked strong feelings in Britain), to twentieth-century counterparts in the aftermath of the world wars and the Cold War, is under assault, whether one looks at Estonia, Taiwan, or a number of other states. These are not separate issues, for the notion of subordination to a greater cause links illiberalism with would-be popularity, and in the domestic and international spheres. An awareness of this cultural, intellectual, and ideological challenge should serve to encourage supporters of liberty to debate policy seriously and to look beyond the short-term politics of electoral cycles, important as those doubtless are.

In looking at change into, and in, the future, it is appropriate to note a range of possible factors, from the technological to the political, the demographic to the cultural. The demographic is possibly the most appropriate when considering populism, because the number of people inherently is, and should be, part of the debate. Alongside ideology, mass is part of the account. Indeed, this is the principal issue with populism on the global scale. All figures for global population are approximate, but the following may be given: 425 million in 1500, one billion in 1804, 1.6 billion in 1900, 2 billion in 1927, 3 billion in 1960, 6 billion in 1999, and 7.3 billion today. All future trends are of course subject to discussion and revision, but the indications in 2015 in the UN DESA report *World Population Prospects: The 2015 Revision*, are for 8.5 billion by 2030, 9.7 by 2025, and, on current trends, at least 11.2 by 2100. Africa is the continent with the greatest likely percentage rise in population, with Nigeria, currently with the seventh largest population in the world, the country in Africa due to rise most, and possibly surpassing the USA to become third by about 2050. The rise in population is certainly a motor of world change, indeed the leading motor, as it is closely linked to the human aspects of climate change; although, of course, other narratives lend themselves to the debate, including, at far longer timespans, geological change, and transformations in the solar system.

Population is the key element of populism, one that can be seen directly, both in the specifics of the Arab nightmare of instability in, and since, 2011 and with reference more generally to the role of the young in revolutionary movements, for example the Russian Revolution of 1917. The usual caveats that are applied to demographic catastrophism relate to the failure of Thomas Malthus to get it right and, more generally, to the ability of technology to deliver a response. The last, however, was most brutally expressed by dictators proclaiming the triumph of humanity in the shape of their power and their remedies. Thus, in China, Mao Zedong rejected the traditional Chinese notion of 'Harmony between the Heavens and Humankind', instead proclaiming 'Man Must Conquer Nature.' Mao himself declared 'Make the high mountain bow its head; make the river yield the way,' and, soon after, in a critique of an essay by Stalin (something always best delivered from a distance), in which Stalin stated that men could not affect natural processes such as geology, Mao claimed 'This argument is incorrect. Man's ability to know and change Nature is unlimited.'

This is dictatorial populism in the most extreme fashion. The supposed good of the people, as interpreted by a disciplined leading section, in the shape of a dictatorial party, is to control all, both human and natural. Indeed, the political attempt to drive environmental issues can be as, or more, extreme and dangerous to human society than the issues presented by climate change. For example, in the Soviet Union, Khrushchev's attempt to cultivate the steppes, in the late 1950s and early 1960s, both failed and greatly affected the local hydrology, harming it in both the short and long terms.

The very bulk of a continually growing *demos* was not the major issue in Classical discussion about the deficiencies of populism. In part, this was because there was no strong trend away from rhythmic patterns of population (and economic) change; there was, instead, a continuous upward trend in population numbers until the second half of the eighteenth century and, even more, the first half of the nineteenth, a trend that continued into the twentieth, and the twenty-first. As a consequence, intellectual, political and ethical thought about the issue was relatively slow to get going. Due to religious concerns and the discrediting of eugenics, it cannot be said that this thought has moved forward other than in bland technocratic solutions linked to family planning. The latter, however, is frequently a classic instance of the moral and practical problems created by putting technical means foremost.

There is clearly more space in the world for human settlement, and technological solutions may well be found to questions of food, water, and fuel availability, waste disposal, mobility, housing, and much else. That does not mean, however, that these solutions will satisfactorily address political, ethnic, and other, tensions linked to resource distribution. That is a neutral phrase for what is very often a rhetoric, if not politics, of redistribution through expropriation and other forms of seizure.

Indeed, one way to look at politics across much of the world today is to see it as a response to the impact of population pressures on living hopes or standards. These pressures can take the form of migration. Trade competition is another form, in that the low-cost of labour, for example in East Asia or South America, owes something to population growth, and, in turn, can help cause deindustrialisation elsewhere. Both instances of these pressures have been significant in the 2010s, although in very different mixes. Concern about change is apt to focus on the challenge to identity offered by large-scale immigration. This was the prime challenge of internationalism to nationalism, and can be seen as an important issue in the expression of English nationalism in the 2010s; although this nationalism was, and is, not so simply defined.

International economic competition and immigration, differing aspects of the same or similar processes, were aspects of the capacity of international relations to fire up populist, or at least popular, concerns. Again, there is a long and complex legacy, for populism can be found in confessional internationalism (international religious movements) in the past and present, notably during the Wars of Religion of the sixteenth century, in debates about international order and justice, and in calls for interventionism. Some have been pernicious, others meritorious. The notion that policy should simply be left to the state, and, in addition, preserved from accountability by secrecy, has many weaknesses. So, yet again, the placing and understanding of populism is unclear: both good and bad, helpful and unhelpful, and, potentially equally so, whether form, means or content. This is of direct relevance for the discussion of English nationalism.

Technology is a different factor, but increases awareness about the world, or, at least, distributes information. There is both a benign and a malign account of technology, as also with populism as a whole. The images of the West transmitted by television, notably to East Germany, are seen as having sapped Communism and contributed to its fall in 1989. It is not surprising that Islamic fundamentalists sought to prevent or limit the spread of information about Western life, or that the Western model was perceived as a threat to them. Television was banned by the Taliban regime in Afghanistan in the 1990s.

Moreover, the internet offered a range and capacity that were different from those of previous national, transnational, and, in particular, global, information and communications systems. The internet also permitted a more engaged and constant consumer response, with, as a result, consumers becoming users, and users becoming producers, as categories were transformed. Media content and software-based products provided platforms for user-driven social interactions and user-generated content (like the dependence of eighteenth-century newspapers on items sent in), rather than being the crucial player in creating content. Wikipedia and Twitter are key instances of user-sourced content.

To some, notably, but definitely not only, in governments, this situation represented information as chaos and crisis. It certainly provided a form and means for populism, one that was different from the rioting mob, but only by so much. Indeed, the application of the word crowd to the internet appeared appropriate. Alongside fears of an Orwellian government, came those of a Hobbesian chaos, with the latter to the fore in 2017–18. This counterpointing reflected the catastrophism and paranoia that characterised much political debate (and right across the political spectrum), but also a lack of intellectual and political purchase in terms of an ability to relate specifics to contexts.

At the same time, one of the sad ironies of the Information Age is that instant access to vast quantities of information, and the explosion of competing voices on the internet, have given many people merely the illusion of being more informed: when one can readily find 'facts' and 'expert opinions' to confirm one's biases, it becomes much easier to distrust any competing views. Possibly that is a definition of populism, that of the rush to judgement. If so, it is scarcely new or specific to particular values, although this rush has been greatly speeded up by the interacting combination of greater literacy, new technology, and the ability and willingness of individuals to spend on the latter. Texts, tweets, Facebook and the internet have amplified a change in sensibility that has been in train for two generations. It has resulted in a fast, 'in your face,' tabloid approach to all sorts of expression including political rhetoric. It is said that people do not need to be educated too deeply as they can always look up information on the internet. However, as people do not know what they do not know, so it is easy to feed them with biased information. They do not have the knowledge to evaluate what they are being told.

At the same time, it is wrong to treat developments in technology in a reductionist fashion. In the 1990s, the Centre Left, notably Bill Clinton and Tony Blair, defined issues and deployed arguments more effectively than the Right, being masters of a certain form of populist politics, in the same way that Donald Trump seeks to be today. On Facebook and television debates, he is skilful at winning attention, and the traditional politicians were pushed onto the defensive during the 2016 presidential campaign.

The entire issue of information and liberalism is given fresh importance by the rate of social change, by the increase in population, which brings larger new generations to the fore, and by the way in which technology is opening up fresh possibilities for a new typology of political space in democratising milieus that, while often highly uncomfortable, are unlikely to go away. Populism as means, rhetoric, and a term of denunciation, both describes and comments on this situation. How to use populist approaches in order to advance and support a range of arguments and interests therefore requires urgent attention across the political spectrum. To bewail populism is probably not the best approach, as that argument is inherently loose and indiscriminate. Condemnation of populism serves the interests of critics rather than assisting informed debate. There is of course the standard approach: 'what I stand for is reasonable, but your approach is crude and populist,' both employed as terms for extreme. The distinction is a nice, not a precise, one, and it is unclear why views that enjoy widespread popular support, notably if they give voice to the otherwise voiceless, are automatically to be dismissed in this fashion. 'Thinking within the box' is, like what is often termed populism, itself comfortable and uncritical. Again, the need for a more acute typology and vocabulary is readily apparent. Each are best if they recognise the strength of nation-states as the basis for identity, while accepting that the state is most benign if subordinate to the nation, and that the nation should be an open community of free individuals.

9

INTO THE FUTURE

England People Very Nice, a thoughtful play by Richard Bean, began a run at the National Theatre in 2009. It drew protestors claiming that its account of immigration was critical of Bangladeshis. Set in Bethnal Green, the play deals with the waves of immigration to this cockpit of the East End. At one level, the play is about assimilation, with immigrants becoming Cockneys, so that the barmaid ends up as a woman of Irish-French extraction married to a Jew and with grandchildren who are half-Bangladeshi. Yet, there are darker currents. There is the backdrop of a xenophobic mob angry at the Huguenots (French Protestants) for taking jobs, the Irish for being Catholics, and the Jews for producing Jack the Ripper (for which there is no evidence), and also accusing the Bangladeshis of being 'curried monkeys.' The British National Party is an ugly element in the story. Even darker are the young Bangladeshis who hate everyone else as infidels and admire Osama bin Laden. The prospect of the Thames running 'with blood' is frequently mentioned in the play. The ability of England to cope with its diversity is left unclear, but room for optimism is limited.

If, despite its far longer and stronger roots, nationalism, as we perceive it, is substantially a modern idea (an approach contested in the earlier chapters), then the modern is always changing. The decline, even reduction, of Britishness led to speculation about the rise of Englishness. There has been much discussion about the possibility of a political outcome for English nationalism, as well as of a cultural outcome. However, at least in the short-term, Englishness has only limited traction. This was seen with the total failure of UKIP, notably in the 2017 general election, and also with limitations in support in England for nationalism. Yet, the lack of strong regionalisms as an alternative to Englishness is instructive. That sits alongside pronounced interest, at least in public policy, in the role of multiculturalism. It is as if identity in a regional form is weak at a time when, instead, public policy is apt to focus, or be focused, on issues of ethnicity, gender and sexuality.

A lack of clarity over place was linked to that over history. Thus, the practice of disputing the national past was in the spotlight in 2013, as revisions to the National Curriculum for history teaching in English and Welsh schools were debated. These disputes echoed earlier differences, and doubtless prefigured those of the future. Aside from the topics to the fore in the consideration of national history, which generally echo the issues most urgent at the time, there were changes to the tone involved. In 2013, David Cameron, in a speech about Britain's position in Europe, reverted to 'Caesar's legions' in arguing that 'We have helped to write European history, and Europe has helped write ours.'

Uncertainty over the past is linked to that over the future. The future nature of Englishness itself is unclear. In part, this is a reflection of uncertainties over the ruralist image. That image can be reconciled to a different reality. For example, the back of the £10 note introduced in 1993 featured Charles Dickens and, as an illustration of his work, the village cricket match from *The*

Pickwick Papers, and not one of the scenes of urban development or life, notably in London, that were far more frequent in his novels. The 2016 replacement, incidentally featuring a misleading image of Jane Austen, more accurately presented a country house, and not one of her urban scenes in Bath or London.

The strength and endurance of the relationship between the ruralist tradition and Englishness derives, in part, from the degree to which the former is not just conservative, but, instead, has been able to accommodate and place the apparently irreconcilable ideals of the Romantic Right (country house, country church, squire, parson, and deferential society) and the Romantic Left (folk society, the village, rural crafts, honest peasantry, and free access for walkers), the latter including the Chartist Land Company. In short, as with cities, there are several ruralist traditions which co-exist.

A comparable sense of place is somewhat lacking for the urban alternative, not least because of the remorseless process of new building and destruction that has affected so much of the urban environment. This is particularly true of the South-East of England where construction has been most extensive. In contrast, cities where population growth has been lowest, for example Liverpool and Glasgow, find it easiest to maintain a distinct identity.

However, ruralism clearly cannot describe the experience of England, the Western society that urbanised first; nor the assumptions and beliefs associated with this urbanisation. The pace of 'development' of rural England, notably the insistence on the building of the very large numbers of new homes, both testifies to the appeal of ruralist ideas of English life, but also greatly threatens them. The urban alternative to this tradition appears to have greater traction with the young. The literary, pictorial, photographic, filmic, and televisual, representation of cities is not one of England as a 'green and pleasant land.' The contrast, in fictional television crime series, between *Midsomer Murders* and city-based series, is readily apparent.

This is a testimony to the fragmented forms of modern Englishness, and thus of English nationalism. Indeed, Englishness is a set of identities, as much clashing as interlocking, rather than an overarching phenomenon. There are significant generational differences as an aspect of the division of both England and Britain by region, class and age. Moreover, the destruction or weakening of traditional benchmarks of national identity, character, and independence, notably in the 1960s, had, and still has, not been followed by the creation of viable alternatives. The same, of course, is true in many other countries and regions. It is unclear whether Britain/England is, or is not, in more difficult circumstances than elsewhere. Possibly the English have less experience of the issues involved due to a more benign history over the last century. With the exception of the Channel Islands in 1940–5, there was no occupation by a foreign military.

Cultural activity provides valuable indications of flux. Current interest in identity in terms of gender, sexuality and ethnicity does not aim to build a central cohesion. Expression of identity, instead, is often a matter of an affirming reaction of other values. This is somewhat different from any attempt to embody traditional wider ideas of Englishness as involving love of fair-play, friendliness, helplfulness to others, concern for the less fortunate, tolerance, and both individualism and the amateur tradition. Whereas, in the 1930s, 1940s and 1950s, films and newsreels offered an optimistic emphasis on social cohesion and patriotism, this is far less the case today, other than, possibly, in terms of the National Health Service, which was founded only in 1948.

Ultimately, Britain, whether a shorthand for Great Britain, or for the United Kingdom, or for the relationship between England and Wales, was created by Acts of Parliament, and can be dissolved by others. The process seems underway in some

INTO THE FUTURE

national institutions. In 2007, BBC Radio 4 dropped the United Kingdom-themed music until then played at the start of broadcasts. The BBC increasingly treats Scotland as different, and watching the news there and listening to political commentary makes this readily apparent.

The future is unclear. The strength of separatist nationalism in Scotland and Wales is uncertain. It is difficult to understand how far it will be possible to reconcile British nationalism, let alone a British identity, with Scottish and Welsh identity. Yet, while to many Scots, England wanted to own a Great Britain, but did not want to be it, other Scots, however, as the referendum in 2014 and the general election in 2017 showed, are enthusiastic for a maintenance of the union. This is even more the case in Wales, despite the effort of Plaid Cymru to copy the SNP. The Welsh flags enthusiastically waved in Cardiff in 2016, when the team did very well in the European football competition, and the repeated talk then of the 'Welsh nation,' did not mean the end of Britain. Within England, nationalism had become more pronounced from the late 1990s, not only at the time of 'Euro 96', but also as manifested in interest in St George's Day.[1] Politically, the latter was adopted as a cause by UKIP. Yet, separatist nationalism gained even less support in England. The Conservative party is a Unionist one, and there is no sign that this will change. Labour and the Liberal Democrats have the same goal, albeit for different reasons.

More profoundly, and over the longer term, the relationship between pressures on society and on the environment, both natural and built, on the one hand, and the popular sense of identity on the other, is complex. Interest in difference, if not nationalism, has led to much more attention being devoted to such a sense in Scotland, Wales and Northern Ireland, than to England. In these three, history, or at least an approach to history, is crucial to particular feelings about what Germans call *Heimat*, which can be loosely translated as homeland. The English counterpart has been partly subsumed or translated into a Britishness, but that does not mean that there is no Englishness.

In both Englishness, and Britishness as understood by the English, the natural and built environments play an inconsistent role. In particular, the notion of the desirable nature of both of these environments held in the North of England, and of the relationship between them, is consciously different from that in the South. In turn, each is carefully differentiated in a local patterning of experience and perception which is increasingly urban. The largest city (or cities) in any region, for example Bristol, Leeds, Manchester, Newcastle and Norwich, are very important to cultural horizons, and, collectively, counterpoint London's long-held dominance. Separately, the post-1970s' new world of 'executive' houses, out-of-town shopping centres, industrial parks and cars (always cars) is at once an Americanised landscape defined in terms of a shared lifestyle, and a setting for distinctive accents and different ethnic mixes. This overlap captures the ambiguous and accumulative character of multiple identities.

Different Englishnesses were to the fore in the 2010s. This process was helped by the concentration of population, prosperity and growth in the South-East. In March 2014, the BBC broadcast a programme 'Mind the Gap: London vs the Rest,' which captured much attention. In June 2014, George Osborne, the Chancellor of the Exchequer and a key political figure from 2010 to 2016, announced in a speech in Manchester, 'the powerhouse of London dominates more and more ... We need a Northern Powerhouse.' He sought to make that a key issue.

Linked to the question of 'the North,' but not restricted to it, there are reasonable questions as to whether the English are less prone to the question of homeland than the Scots, Welsh, or Northern Irish; and whether the key element within England is regional, which was the theme of the Blair government, or national. Conversely, immigration has had much resonance as an issue in part due to English nationalism, or, at least, consciousness. In addition, the Brexit vote had a very high correlation with 'English, not British' identity in England. In *A Legacy of Spies* (2017), John Le Carré juxtaposed Europe not with Britain but with England. The all-wise George Smiley, tracked down in retirement in Freiburg, considers the purpose of his life in espionage:

> So was it all for *England*, then? ... There was a time, of course there was. But *whose* England? *Which* England? England all alone, a citizen of nowhere? I'm a European, Peter. If I had a mission—if I was ever aware of one beyond our business with the enemy, it was to Europe. ... If I had an unattainable ideal, it was of leading Europe out of her darkness towards a new age of reason.[2]

Given that England was largely responsible for the vote against the EU in 2016, the choice of this juxtaposition appears apt. Made necessary by the rise of the SNP, Englishness is now an issue thanks to the EU.

English identity is apparently slowly emerging from the catch-all British identity, now that the Scots, Welsh, and Northern Irish, especially the Scots, are vocally asserting their identity, and Brexit has provided a fresh opportunity. The growing intertwining of the British question and Brexit at the close of 2017 has complicated debates about the future situation of parts of the United Kingdom, notably over the Irish question. As Dennis Staunton, London editor of the *Irish Times*, pointed out, the 1998 Good Friday Agreement

> has been sustained by a kind of constructive ambiguity that has allowed each community in Northern Ireland to interpret it in their own way. Northern Irish citizens can be British or Irish or both, a concept that made little difference as long as the UK and Ireland were in the EU. Brexit has cast a harsh light on that ambi-

guity, forcing the people of Northern Ireland into being British or European.[3]

In practice, such ambiguity was central (as in other countries) to the issue of multiple identity; and, therefore, was not inherently a problem other than when changes led to a need to confront (or avoid confrontation) with this issue. In essence, change had been pushed to the fore from the 1990s, with the Scottish Parliament and Welsh Assembly, and, subsequently, in the 2010s, first with the Scottish independence referendum and then with Brexit. This process ensured that discussion of English nationalism was heavily politicised and in very immediate contexts, but the same was more generally true of other nationalisms as well, and will go on being the case.

Looked at from a different direction, the end, or rather lessening, of ambiguity was an aspect of a change in politics, as the lack of a clear constitution was replaced by a process of constitution-making. This was one respect in which, having, in part due to the success in the Second World War, avoided the major constitutional and political transformation that most other European states experienced in the 1940s, Britain in the 2010s was increasingly affected by developments that would have been familiar there, including the politicisation of justice and policing, and a divisiveness in politics that affected social, cultural, and other links, including the discussion of history.

That situation was not one in which it would be possible to reach a consensus about English nationalism, or indeed anything political, social, cultural or economic. That, however, is not the same as arguing that issues and answers cannot exist, but only to say that they will not be abstracted from the process of contention that is inherent both to democracy and to an educated electorate. Thus, turning on its head the claim that contention, as after the Brexit referendum, reflected ignorance, can come the view that it arose because many people held views that reflected their attempt to formulate, articulate, and act on responses. So also, for example, with the discussion over the future of the Labour Party.

Indeed, it was ironic that there was criticism of a lack of popular engagement with politics, yet when such engagement did occur—whether support for Brexit or for a more radical Labour Party, or for both—it was bitterly criticised. This raised questions not only about political culture, but also concerning legitimation. Leaving aside claims about a lack of true commitment to democracy or democratisation on the part of these critics, there was the complex relationship between ideal and expediency that affects so much of politics, as well as the process of selective rhetoric. Addressing ambiguity strongly raised the latter, and did so in a context in which a willingness to compromise diminished. Indeed, 2014 onwards saw a marked rise in partisanship in British politics. The process was particularly apparent in Scotland in 2014–15 and in England from 2015. The abuse and threats visited on politicians rose markedly, a situation seen tragically with the assassination of Jo Cox, MP, in 2016 during the referendum campaign, and, far more commonly, with abuse and intimidation during the 2017 election. In part, this situation underlined the problem posed by the issue of English nationalism, although the abuse and intimidation of politicians and canvassers in the 2017 election came disproportionately from the Left. The far-Right, for example in the person of Cox's assassin, found it easy to articulate an ideology of nationalism, albeit an empty one other than of paranoid sensitivities, destructive spleen, and violence. The lack of an effective discussion of English nationalism by the political parties was a particular problem. There are Scottish and Welsh Tories and Labour etc., but not English equivalents, which, unfortunately, leaves much of the English political space for defining nationalism to the far-Right, itself an aspect of a broader problem with political identity. This is not only unfortunate; it is intellectually flawed and the Achilles heel of British politics.

Yet any process of asserting English or British identity, however valuable and natural, appears to be vexed and to lead to criticism, which is sometimes extremely strident. This approach underlines points about a freedom to disagree. A discussion in late 2017 about the need to 'involve history teachers tutoring pupils in key events in the development of British democracy, such as Magna Carta' caused controversy, with one London headmistress, Vicky Bingham, declaring that the curriculum sounds 'ineffective in rooting out radical terrorism. The idea of pupils coming together in mutual understanding because they all know our island story sounds ... slightly jingoistic ... the idea that Britain has some special claim to democracy smacks of hubris.' This is ironic and ignorant, as it is in practice correct that it has such a claim. Earlier in 2017, Amanda Spielman, the Chief Inspector of Schools, had warned in a speech to Birmingham schools that they should all teach British values.[4]

In part, the critique is due to unhappiness with the idea of nationalism as opposed to identity. Also in 2017, Sir Peter Luff, a former Conservative minister and then the Chairman of the National Heritage Lottery Board, distinguished between Englishness, about which he was positive, and 'the English nationalism part of Englishness,' concerning which he was very anxious.[5]

Possibly this is an aspect of uneasiness about the emergence of nationhood. That has never been a contention-free process. There is also the (separate) extent to which some who were anyway uneasy about aspects of Britishness have extrapolated this concern in discussing Englishness. Secondly, supporters of Britishness can criticise Englishness. There is unease among backers of Englishness about particular interpretations of the latter. Separately, there is also a thrashing of nationalism as an aspect of the 'culture wars,' and, more generally, as part of a political or politicised critique of Conservatives and conservatism. This approach can look for deep historical roots for what is disliked, as with the unconvincing argument that there is a 'continuity in English racism from the Anglo-Saxon landings, through the establishment of English hegemony, up to the present day.'[6]

Linked to these issues is the effectiveness of the nation-state as a representative political unit, a debate characterised by a kind of circularity: the nation-state represents national interests effectively because its very existence *defines* those interests. What is less clear is that the interests thus defined and pursued by the nation-state are the primary interests of the people of that state. However, given that these interests do not exist clearly, except in the most basic terms, outside the political process, the nation-state plays a crucial role in the discussion, defining, validating, and forwarding of such interests.

The context of this activity clearly varies, with the range offered being international to regional. That variation helps account for present-day anger as well as the confusion on which anger so often draws. Indeed, it is precisely because of the role of historical formation in giving identities and meaning to the lives of political communities that the present conjuncture is so significant. If, as argued in this book, Britishness is historically specific, notably linked in its establishment to developments from 1588 to 1746, then the same may be true of Englishness. This is the case whether Scotland leaves Britain, as appeared possible in 2014, and may well, if the SNP has its way, recur as an issue; or, whether, within a more instrumental Britain still including Scotland, it is otherwise necessary to define England. This may be pushed rapidly to the fore as the result of a possible federal deal that emerges from some future government supported by nationalist votes, for example a Labour-SNP or Labour-Plaid

Cymru arrangement after the next election which is due in 2022 at the latest.

This point further raises the question of the often conflicting 'rights' of the majority and minority. For example, should the majority of Britons have had a say in the Scottish minority's referendum? They did, in the shape of parliamentary approval, but does that suffice? What about the 'rights' of the minorities if they take the shape of the constituent countries, and how does that include England? What does 'rights' mean in this context? A federal deal may be the solution offered by a Labour government supported by SNP votes, *if* one emerges from the next election. Britishness would then become a residual framework, but also a continuing obstacle to any English or Scottish independence.

The situation is complex and nuanced. It is crucially important to neglect neither the contingent, in the shape of the pressures of domestic and international developments; nor continuities, most obviously in terms of institutional, constitutional and political longevities. The significance of the former has been underlined by the multiple unpredictabilities of British politics since 2014. Indeed, the counterfactual is now hardwired into much discussion of recent and current politics, as, indeed, it should be. This point underlines the impetus given to English nationalism by the strength of Scottish nationalism, a reflection of the tenth-century response to Danish invasion. Both English and Scottish nationalism, and notably the latter, challenge the overlap between English and British identity. This overlap is part of the multi-layered nature of the identity of the English, which has long worked for them and that currently does so for most of them.

Returning to the simplistic, but also helpful, issue, or, at least rhetoric, of 'somewhere' and 'anywhere,'[7] the attempt to displace the nation-state from its position in popular loyalties faces major difficulties. This issue is complicated, if not confused, by whether the nation-state is Britain or England; but the inherent issue is the same. A sense of place and continuity is crucial to the harmony of individuals and societies. It is challenged by the continual process of change, one that entails the alteration, invention and reinvention of traditions. Except in periods when there is a stress on the value of a break with the past, change is in large part acceptable to much of the population only if it does not disrupt too sharply their sense of identity, community and continuity.

Today, globalisation is an important aspect of the change and a major part of the rhetoric. As a concept, it captures the tension between 'somewhere' and 'anywhere,' because the world has consistently proved a difficult unit and agency for populations to identify with. It is at once too diffuse and too much an expression of contentious views as to interests and policies. The issue, or, rather bundle of issues, of the acceptability of change vary across the world, and involve subjective judgements; but it is no less important for that reason.

10

POSTSCRIPT FROM A PUB

One of the features of English life that Orwell would have noted was the pub. In practice, this source and expression of cohesion is becoming much less common. Statistics vary, but those produced by the British Beer and Pub Association (BBPA) indicate 67,800 in the UK in 1982, but only 50,800 in 2015. In the early 1970s, there were 75,000. The Campaign for Real Ale (CAMRA) claimed in September 2017 that the number had fallen to 47,000, with thirty-one closing per week. The number of pubs per capita has fallen more rapidly. Possibly that is just a simple indication of change, but the replacements—communication by social media and the drinking at home of alcohol obtained in supermarkets—suggest a more fractured social patterning. The former, in particular, poses challenges to conventional forms of community.

Pubs also offer a form of continuity, although that can be patchy. When I asked four young men in the pub The Waterloo Cross on 3 September 2008 what the pub (located near the Wellington Monument in Somerset) was named after, none was forthcoming. One thought the name was something to do with

Napoleon. Wellington did not feature, which was an ironic commentary on the claim in Gilbert and Sullivan's *Iolanthe* (1882) that 'every child can tell' that Wellington had thrashed Napoleon. Since 2008, The Prince Blucher, a pub in Tiverton named after Blücher, Wellington's Prussian ally at Waterloo, has closed.

The potential nature of pub Englishness is captured by The Windsor Castle in the Heavitree area of Exeter. The Cross of St George flies over the pub, which, on the outside, bears the motto 'The Locals' Local.' It is fair to say that, as with many pubs, The Windsor Castle has an older clientele. It is a world away from the gastro-pubs and student nightspots of the city. Interestingly, interviews in the latter two do not show much sense of what Englishness means or can mean, and also little real understanding of alternatives that can unite more than a fraction of the population.

In 2002, Richard Weight referred to 'a myopic intellectual elite, unwilling to weave England's many-splendoured features into a coherent, progressive picture around which the country could unite.'[1] Possibly coherence is an unrealistic assumption, and unity certainly cannot be expected in a modern democratic society. However, his complaint is in part justified. Having argued for long that states are artificial constructions, intellectuals have failed to confront the issue that England exists, and that its role and character are being pushed to the fore as the stability of the United Kingdom comes under increasing pressure, notably from the ambitions of Scottish nationalism. English nationalism is too important to be left to the extremists.

NOTES

1. INTRODUCTION

1. R. Winder, 'After Brexit, England will have to rethink its identity,' *Guardian*, 8 Jan. 2016.
2. J. Andrews, *Letters to a Young Gentleman on His Setting Out for France* (London, 1784), p. 126.
3. D. Woolf, 'A Feminine Past? Gender, Genre, and Historical Knowledge in England, 1500–1800,' *American Historical Review*, 102 (1997), pp. 634–79; K. O'Brien, *Women and the Enlightenment in Eighteenth-Century Britain* (Cambridge, 2009).
4. H. More, *Strictures on the Modern System of Female Education* (London, 1799).
5. R. Colls, *Identity of England* (Oxford, 2002); J. Paxman, *The English: A Portrait of a People* (London, 1998); R. Scruton, *England: An Elegy* (London, 2000); K. Kumar, *The Making of English National Identity* (London, 2003); R. Hatsell (ed.), *The English Question* (Manchester, 2006); P. Parrinder, *Nation and Novel: The English Novel from Its Origins to the Present Day* (Oxford, 2006); C. Westall and M. Gardiner, *Literature of an Independent England* (Basingstoke, 2013); M. Kenny, *The Politics of English Nationhood* (Oxford, 2014); R. Tombs, *the English and Their History* (London, 2015).

2. THE OLD ENGLISH STATE

1. Chauncy, *Antiquities* (London, 1700), p. 1.
2. J. Blair, *Building Anglo-Saxon England* (Princeton, NJ, 2018). I would

like to thank John Blair for sharing with me part of this work pre-publication.

3. J. Blair, *The Church in Anglo-Saxon Society* (Oxford, 2005), pp. 23, 507.

4. N.J. Higham, *Ecgfrith: King of the Northumbrians, High-King of Britain* (Donington, 2015).

5. M. Molyneaux, *The Formation of the English Kingdom in the Tenth Century* (Oxford, 2015).

6. C. Insley, '"Ottonians with Pipe Rolls"? Political Culture and Performance in the Kingdom of the English, *c.* 900–*c.* 1050,' *History*, 102 (2017), pp. 772–86.

7. C.G. Robertson and J.G. Bartholomew, *Historical and Modern Atlas of the British Empire*, pp. v-vi, 10.

8. J. Campbell, 'The late Anglo-Saxon state: a maximum view,' *Proceedings of the British Academy*, 87 (1994), pp. 39–65.

9. G. Molyneux, 'Why were some tenth-century English kings presented as rulers of Britain?,' *Transactions of the Royal Historical Society*, 6ᵗʰ ser., 21 (2011), pp. 59–91.

10. E. Kedourie, *Nationalism* (London, 1960), p. 1; E. Hobsbawn, *Nations and Nationalism since 1780: Programme, Myth, Reality* (2ⁿᵈ edn, Manchester, 1993) and (ed.), *The Oxford Handbook of the History of Nationalism* (Oxford, 2013).

11. A.D. Smith, *The Ethnic Origins of Nations* (Oxford, 1986), pp. 22–30, *The Nation in History* (Cambridge, 2000), and *The Antiquity of Nations* (Cambridge, 2004).

12. Molyneaux, *English Kingdom*, pp. 233–49.

13. Blair, *Building Anglo-Saxon England*, conclusion.

3. LINKED TO FRANCE, 1066–1453

1. C. Wickham, 'Problems of Comparing Rural Societies in Early Medieval Western Europe,' *TRHS*, 6ᵗʰ series, II (1992), pp. 242, 236.

2. A. Macfarlane, *The Origins of English Individualism: The Family, Property and Social Transition* (Oxford, 1978), pp. 165, 175, and 'The cradle of capitalism,' in J. Baechler, J.A. Hall and M. Mann (eds), *Europe and the Rise of Capitalism* (Oxford, 1988), pp. 185–203.

3. S.F.C. Milsom, *Historical Foundations of the Common Law* (1969).

4. D. Goodhart, *The Road to Somewhere: The Populist Revolt and the Future of Politics* (London, 2017).

5. J. Watts, *The Making of Polities: Europe, 1300–1500* (Cambridge, 2009).

6. A. Butterfield, *The Familiar Enemy: Chaucer, Language and Nation in the Hundred Years War* (Oxford, 2009); D. Matthews, *Writing to the King: Nation, Kingship, and Literature in England, 1250–1350* (Cambridge, 2010); J. Good, *The Cult of St George in Medieval England* (Woodbridge, 2009).

7. R. Frame, *The Political Development of the British Isles, 1100–1400* (Oxford, 1990), p. 179; P. Meyvaert, '"Rainaldus est malus scriptor Francigenus"—Voicing national antipathy in the Middle Ages', *Speculum*, 66 (1991), pp. 743–63.

8. M. Carruthers (ed.), *Language in Medieval Britain: Networks and Exchanges* (Donington, 2015).

4. THE NEW NATIONALISM, 1453–1603

1. D.S. Gehring, *Anglo-German Relations and the Protestant Cause: Elizabethan Foreign Policy and Pan-Protestantism* (London, 2013).

2. Sir Thomas Smith, *De Republica Anglorum*, edited by L. Alston (Cambridge, 1906).

3. Scene 18. G. Taylor, J. Jowett, T. Bourus, and G. Egan (eds), *The New Oxford Shakespeare. The Complete Works* (Oxford, 2017), p. 354.

4. M. Gove, 'A drum roll, please. Britons are back as heroes at long last.' *Times*, 6 Nov. 2007, section 2, p. 8.

5. C.M. Petto, *Mapping and Charting in Early Modern England and France* (Lanham, MD., 2015).

5. BRITISH ENGLAND, 1603–1783

1. C. Hill, *God's Englishman: Oliver Cromwell and the English Revolution* (London, 1970).

2. K. Morgan, ed., *An American Quaker in the British Isles: The Travel Journals of Jabez Maud Fisher, 1775–1779* (Oxford, 1992).

3. D. DeWispelare, *Multilingual Subjects: On Standard English, Its Speakers, and Others in the Long Eighteenth Century* (Philadelphia, PA., 2017);

J. Sorensen, *How Eighteenth-Century Slang, Cant, Provincial Languages, and Nautical Jargon Became English* (Princeton, NJ, 2017).

4. M. Riley and A.D. Smith (eds), *Nation and Classical Music from Handel to Copland* (Woodbridge, 2016).

5. T.W. Perry, *Public Opinion, Propaganda, and Politics in Eighteenth-Century England. A Study of the Jew Bill of 1753* (Cambridge, MA, 1962).

6. Adams, *Works* (edited by) C.F. Adams, III, 394–6; J. Boyd (ed.), *Papers of Thomas Jefferson*, IX, 364–5.

7. Echard, *History*, II, 1.

8. Ibid., II, 910.

9. G. Lyttelton, *Letters from a Persian in England* (4th edn, London, 1735), pp. 179–98.

10. J. Black, *A Subject for Taste: Culture in Eighteenth-Century England* (London, 2005).

6. ENGLISHNESS AND EMPIRE, 1783–1967

1. E. Burke, *Revolutionary Writings*, edited by I. Hampsher-Monk (Cambridge, 2014), p. 34.

2. H. Chisick, *The Limits of Reform in the Enlightenment: Attitudes towards the Education of the Lower Classes in Eighteenth-Century France* (Princeton, NJ, 1981). For a recent more positive view of the Enlightenment, S. Pinker, *Enlightenment Now: The Case for Reason, Science, Humanism and Progress* (London, 2018).

3. I. Hampsher-Monk, 'Edmund Burke in the Tory World,' in J. Black (ed.), *The Tory World: Deep History and the Tory Theme in British Foreign Policy, 1679–2014* (Farnham, 2015), pp. 83–101; E. Jones, *Edmund Burke and the Invention of Modern Conservatism, 1830–1914* (Oxford, 2017).

4. E. Nares, *Burghley* (London, 1828), pp. xx-xxii.

5. W. Hutchinson, *Cumberland*, I, 1–7. For the background, S. Smiles, *Ancient Britain and the Romantic Imagination* (New Haven, CT., 1994).

6. J. Wyld, *Notes to Accompany Mr Wyld's Model of the Earth, Leicester Square* (London, 1851).

7. W.V. Harris, *Roman Power: A Thousand Years of Empire* (Cambridge, 2016).

8. D.W. Hayton, 'Lewis Namier: Nationality, Territory and Zionism' *International Journal of Politics, Culture and Society*, 30 (2017), pp. 171–82.
9. S. Badsey, 'Great Britain,' in 1914–1918 Online International Encyclopaedia of the First World War, https://encyclopedia.1914–1918-online.net/themes
10. M. Burrows, *Foreign Policy*, pp. 32–5.
11. A. Ward and G.P. Gooch (eds), *The Cambridge History of British Foreign Policy 1783–1919*, I (Cambridge, 1922), pp. 38–9.
12. *Encyclopaedia Britannica* (Edinburgh, 1815), VIII, 44.
13. E.g. R. Barr, *The Triumphs of Eugene Valmont* (1906, Harpenden 2015 edition), pp. 49, 63.
14. F. Hume, 'The Ghost's Touch,' in M. Edwards (ed.), *Crimson Snow: Winter Mysteries* (London, 2016), p. 15.
15. *Times*, 15 April 1905. See, more generally, R. Toye, *Churchill's Empire: The World That Made Him and the World He Made* (London, 2010).
16. D. Blair, *Dinkum Diggers: An Australian Battalion at War* (Carlton, Victoria, 2001).
17. T. Cook, *At the Sharp End: Canadians Fighting the Great War, 1914–1916* (Toronto, 2007) and *Shock Troops: Canadians Fighting the Great War, 1917–1918* (Toronto, 2008).
18. P. Williamson, *Stanley Baldwin: Conservative Leadership and National Values* (Cambridge, 2007).
19. J. Stapleton, *Sir Arthur Bryant and National Identity in Twentieth-Century Britain* (London, 2005).
20. A. McLaren, *Playboys and Mayfair Men: Crime, Class, Masculinity, and Fascism in 1930s London* (Baltimore, MD, 2017).
21. J.M. Tregenza, *Professor of Democracy: The Life of Charles Henry Pearson* (Melbourne, 1968).
22. Pearson, *Historical Maps* (London, 1869), pp. v-vii.
23. J. Marsh, *Back to the Land: The Pastoral Impulse in Victorian England from 1880 to 1914* (London, 1982), pp. 245–7; P. Harrington, 'Holst and Vaughan Williams: Radical Pastoral,' in C. Norris (ed.), *Music and the Politics of Culture* (London, 1989), pp. 106–27; R. Stradling and M. Hughes, *The English Musical Renaissance, 1860–1940: Construction and Deconstruction* (London, 1993), pp. 60–8.

24. M. Bartholomew, *In Search of H.V. Morton* (London, 2004).

25. E. Buettner, *Europe after Empire: Decolonisation, Society, and Culture* (Cambridge, 2016).

26. B. Grob-Fitzgibbon, *Continental Drift: Britain and Europe from the End of Empire to the Rise of Euroscepticism* (New York, 2016).

27. R. Weight, *Patriots: National Identity in Britain 1940–2000* (London, 2002), p. 135.

7. ENGLISHNESS AND THE DECLINE OF BRITISHNESS, 1968–2018

1. S. Pincus, '"To Protect English Liberties": the English Nationalist Revolution of 1688–1689,' in T. Claydon and I. McBride (eds), *Protestantism and National Identity: Britain and Ireland, c.1650–c.1850* (Cambridge, 1998), p. 102.

2. L. Bruce, 'Beef for Christmas,' *Tatler and Bystander* (8 November 1957).

3. R. Tombs, 'Non, le Brexit, n'est pas seulement l'expression du nationalisme anglais,' *Le Monde*, 23 Nov. 2017, p. 12.

4. P. Manent, 'Le gouvernants ne nous représentent plus, il nous surveillent,' *Le Figaro*, 1 Aug. 2016, p. 19.

5. C.A. Hagerman, *British Imperial Muse: The Classics, Imperialism and the Indian Empire, 1784–1914* (Basingstoke, 2013).

6. J. Kent, *William Temple: Church, State and Society in Britain, 1880–1950* (Cambridge, 1992).

7. E. Carpenter, *Archbishop Fisher: His Life and Times* (Norwich, 1991); A. Chandler and D. Hein, *Archbishop Fisher, 1945–1961: Church, State and World* (Farnham, 2012).

8. D. Bull, *Football and the Common People* (1994).

9. L.J. Colley, *Acts of Union and Disunion* (London, 2014).

10. B. Wellings, *English Nationalism and Euroscepticism: Losing the Peace* (Bern, 2012).

11. Prime Minister's Questions, 21 May 2003, *Hansard*, 405, no. 99, columns 1004–5, 1012–13.

12. D. Gover and M. Kenny, *Finding the Good in EVEL: An evaluation of 'English Votes for English Laws' in the House of Commons* (London, 2016).

13. F. Geary and T. Stark, 'What Happened to Regional Inequality in

Britain in the Twentieth Century?,' *Economic History Review*, 69 (2016), pp. 215–28.

14. R. Wendorf, *Growing Up Bookish: An Anglo-American Memoir* (New Castle, DE, 2017), pp. 138–9.

15. D. Marquand, 'Britain's problem is not with Europe, but with England,' *Guardian*, 19 December 2017.

16. D. Marquand, *The End of the West: The Once and Future Europe* (Princeton, NJ, 2011).

17. D. Aaronovitch, 'Our Island Must Stop Living in the Tudor Past,' *Times*, 24 Jan. 2013, p. 21. For the use of Shakespeare by a Eurosceptic, see B. Cash, 'Rotten Parchment Bonds,' *European Journal*, 12, 2 (Feb. 2005), p. 2.

18. J. Black, *Clio's Battles. Historiography in Practice* (Bloomington, IN, 2015). See also *Contesting History: Narratives of Public History* (London, 2014).

19. P. Stocker, *English Uprising: Brexit and the Mainstreaming of the Far Right* (New York, 2018).

8. POPULISM

1. T.G. Otte, 'Die zwei Gesichter des Populismus: populismus und die Zähmung der Demokratie im modernen Grossbritannien,' in T. Beigel and G. Eckert (eds), *Populismus: Varianten von Volksherrschaft in Geschichte und Gegenwart* (Münster, 2017), pp. 240–54.

2. R. McKibbin, 'The Fragmentation of the Two-Party System in British Politics, *c.* 1950–2015,' *20th Century British History*, 27 (2016), pp. 450–69.

3. E. Luce, *The Retreat of Western Liberalism* (London, 2017).

4. O. Jones, *Chavs: The Demonization of the Working Class* (London, 2011).

9. INTO THE FUTURE

1. Weight, *Patriots*, pp. 708–13.

2. J. Le Carré, *A Legacy of Spies* (London, 2017), p. 262.

3. D. Staunton, 'Irony of Brexit, that it pushes us closer to a united Ireland,' *Evening Standard*, 5 Dec. 2017, p. 17.

4. Sian Griffiths, 'Head denounces "jingoistic lessons in British values,"' *Sunday Times*, 5 Nov. 2017, p. 16.

5. Luff to Black, email, 5 Nov. 2017.

6. D. Banham, 'Anglo-Saxon attitudes: in search of the origins of English racism,' *European Review of History*, 1 (1994), p. 155.

7. D. Goodhart, *The Road to Somewhere: The Populist Revolt and the Future of Politics* (London, 2017).

10. POSTSCRIPT FROM A PUB

1. R. Weight, *Patriots: National Identity in Britain 1940–2000* (London, 2002), p. 726.

INDEX

INDEX

Baldwin of Flanders, Count: 35–6

Balfour Act (1902): provisions of, 120

Barker, Ernest: *Character of England, The* (1947), 129

Barr, Robert: 115

Bartholomew, J.G.: *Historical and Modern Atlas of the British Empire* (1905), 32

BBC History Magazine: 46

Bean, Richard: *England People Very Nice*, 179

Becket, Thomas: Archbishop of Canterbury, 47

Bede: *Ecclesiastical History of the English People* (731), 28

Benn, Tony: 140

Benson, Arthur: 'Land of Hope and Glory', 8

Berners-Lee, Tim: 46

Betjeman, John: 126

Bill of Rights (1689): 85

Bingham, Vicky: 188

Blackstone, William: 104; *Commentaries on the Laws of England* (1765–9), 97

Blair, Tony: 15, 177; administration of, 148, 184–5

Bolsheviks: German support for, 122

Bonaparte, Napoleon: 14, 108, 193–4

Boniface of Savoy: Archbishop of Canterbury, 48

Boudica: 22

Brexit Referendum (2016): 3, 5–6, 15, 141, 144–6, 168–9, 185–6; political impact of, 158; voting patterns of, 161, 168

Britain First: founding of (2011), 157

Britart: 147

British Beer and Pub Association (BBPA): 193

British Broadcasting Corporation (BBC): 161; 'Mind the Gap: London vs the Rest' (2014), 184; Radio 4, 140, 157, 183; *Today*, 158

British Empire: 10, 16–17, 102, 111, 119, 125, 144; decline of, 132–4, 145; role in British identity, 8

British identity/Britishness: 11, 77, 148, 180, 184; development of, 83; imperial, 112, 134; language of, 15; qualification of, 131; relationship with Englishness, 110–11; role of British Empire in, 8; supporters of, 188–9

British National Party (BNP): 179; members of, 157

British Union of Fascists (BUF): members of, 123

Britpop: 147

Brown, Gordon: 15

Burgundy: 56

Burke, Edmund: 104–6, 139–40; *Appeal from the New to the Old*

INDEX

INDEX

INDEX

INDEX

INDEX

Huguenots: 61; immigration of, 89; repression of, 87

Hume, Ferguson Wright: 115

Hundred Years' War (1337–1453): 9, 27, 53, 55–6, 60; Battle of Agincourt (1415), 54; Battle of Crécy (1346), 53; Battle of Halidon Hill (1333), 53; Battle of Neville's Cross (1346), 53; Battle of Poitiers (1356), 72–3; Siege of Calais (1346–7), 110; Treaty of Troyes (1420), 54

Hungary: 163; Budapest, 10

Hunter, Alan: *Landed Gently* (1957), 133

Hutchinson, William: *History of the Country of Cumberland* (1794), 109

Iberian Union (1580–1640): 78; collapse of (1640), 10; Portuguese Restoration War (1640–68), 10

immigration: 7, 118, 146–7, 174; Irish, 124, 131; large-scale, 15, 174; limits on, 124; opposition to, 145

imperialism: British, 19, 32

India: Independence of (1947), 15, 132–3

Industrial Revolution: 102, 159

Information Age: 176

Innocent III, Pope: interdict imposed on England (1208), 47–8

Inquisition: 114

Interregnum (1649–60): 107

Iraq: Operation Iraqi Freedom (2003–14), 133

Ireland: 36, 41, 46, 86–7, 90, 102 110–11, 117, 121, 140–1, 148; Great Famine, 116

Ireland Act (1949): 122

Irish Free State: 122

Irish Times: 185

Irving, Washington: 115

Islam: 46, 143; fundamentalist, 175; radical, 15

Israel: 82, 167

Italy: 26, 43, 132, 167; Rome, 62, 64, 66; Unification (1815–71), 171

Jack Cade Rebellion (1450): 165

Jackson's Oxford Journal: 99

Jacobite Rebellions (1715–16/1745–6): 67, 71, 88, 96, 125–6; defeat of (1746), 84

James I of England: 73; accession of (1603), 10, 77–8

James II of England: 71, 82, 85, 104; expulsion of (1688–9), 13, 87

Japan: 8, 10; land reform in, 166

Jefferson, Thomas: 89

Jesuits: 114

jingoism: 133

John, King: 17, 46, 49, 62, 116

Johnson, Samuel: 22; *Dictionary*, 96

INDEX

INDEX

Manent, Pierre: 141

Manson, James Bolivar: 127

Mao Zedong: 173

Margaret: 77

Marlborough, Duke of (John Churchill): 9

Marquand, David: 159–60; background of, 160

Marr, Andrew: 161

Marxism: 169

Mary, Queen of Scots: 78

Mary Tudor: 79, 110; family of, 78; re-Catholicisation under, 67

Mary II, Queen: 22, 83

Matilda: 40

May Day Riot (1517): 165

McDonnell, A.G.: *England, Their England* (1933), 144

Medieval Scots Law: 44

Merkel, Angela: 162

Midsomer Murders: 182

Millennium Dome: 142

Milton, John: 160

Minot, Laurence: 53

Mitford, Nancy: *Love in a Cold Climate* (1949), 130

Mitterand, François: 162

Modernism: 127

Montagu, Elizabeth: 96–7

Montesquieu: 98

Moore, Sir John: 9

Moorhouse, E. Hallam: 121

More, Thomas: execution of (1535), 65

Morton, H.V.: *In Search of England* (1927), 128–9

Mosley, Oswald: leader of BUF, 123

Mowbray, Lord: 140

Napoleonic Wars (1803–15): 8–9, 103, 108; Battle of Waterloo (1815), 194; Hundred Days (1815), 8; Trafalgar Campaign (1805), 14, 140

Nares, Edward: writings of, 107–8

National Association for the Vindication of Scottish Rights: launch of (1853), 111–12

National Health Service (NHS): 139, 159, 182; formation of, 143

National Heritage Lottery Board: 188

National Library of Scotland: 149

National Museum of Scotland: 149

National Theatre: 179

National Trust: 147; founding of (1895), 127

nationalism: 1–4, 8–9, 20, 23, 27, 35–6, 48, 80, 82–3, 89, 91–2, 95, 103, 122, 141, 143–4, 159–60, 174; British, 121, 145; Cornish, 151; definitions of, 48; English, 2, 6–7, 20–1, 29, 33, 35, 50, 55, 59–60, 62, 64, 67, 71, 83, 105, 118, 130, 144–7, 153–4, 156, 165, 167,

INDEX

Troubles, The (*c.* 1960–98): Good Friday Agreement (1998), 185–6

Trump, Donald: 167–8, 177

Tudor Revolution in Government: 42

Turkey: 171

Turner, Sharon: *History of England* (1799–1805), 109

Twitter: 175

UEFA Euro 96: 146

UK Independence Party (UKIP): 161; electoral performance of (2010), 155; electoral performance of (2017), 156, 180; failure of, 180; founding of (1993), 154; ideology of, 156–7, 183; members of, 156

United Kingdom of Great Britain and Northern Ireland (UK): 1–2, 4, 10–11, 14–19, 34, 55, 64, 73, 82–3, 85, 87–9, 115–16, 134, 137, 148, 157, 166, 182–3; creation of, 11, 83–4, 122; idea of, 91; literary tradition of, 19; nuclear arsenal of, 133; Scottish independence within, 111; Victorian, 9

United Nations (UN): Department of Economic and Social Affairs (DESA), 172; *World Population Prospects: The 2015 Revision*, 172

United States of America (USA): 50, 133, 144, 172; Civil Rights Movement, 166; Hollywood, 18–19; New Deal, 7; War of Independence (1775–83), 7, 89

University of London: Queen Mary College, 3

urbanisation: 102, 117, 171, 181; mass, 171

Valmont, Eugène: 115

Veritas: ideology of, 154

Victoria, Queen: 117–18

Vietnam War (1955–75): 140

Vikings: 109, 146

Voltaire: 98

Wales: 2, 4, 7, 10, 26, 34, 36, 46, 83, 86, 90, 110–11, 116, 119–21, 123, 125, 148, 157, 159, 162, 182; as political unit, 11; Cardiff, 183; Gwynedd, 34; Hawarden, 112

War of the Austrian Succession (1740–8): 8

War of the League of Cambrai (1508–16): Battle of Flodden (1513), 77

War of the Quadruple Alliance (1718–20): 8

War of the Roses (1455–1487): 62, 74

War of the Spanish Succession (1702–13): 8

Warner, Sylvia Townsend: *Lolly Willowes* (1926), 130

INDEX